ASIAN NEUTRALISM
AND U.S. POLICY

ASIAN NEUTRALISM
AND U.S. POLICY

Sheldon W. Simon

American Enterprise Institute for Public Policy Research
Washington, D. C.

Sheldon W. Simon is professor of political science and chairman of the department of political science at Arizona State University.

327. 0 95

Si 5 a

94 96 0

OLT 1975

ISBN 0-8447-3166-8

Foreign Affairs Study No. 21, August 1975

Library of Congress Catalog Card No. 75-13644

Printed in the United States of America

To Alex

CONTENTS

PREFACE

This monograph grew out of a research-lecture trip through Asia in the spring and summer of 1973 under the auspices of the United States Information Service (USIS), with additional support from the University of Kentucky and the Institute of International Relations of the University of British Columbia. (The radio broadcast and foreign language press translations included here were taken from the Foreign Broadcast Information Service *Daily Reports* dealing with the People's Republic of China, the Soviet Union, the Asia-Pacific area, and South Asia.) The purpose of the trip was to interview Asian academics and Asian foreign affairs officials about their concepts of regional security and their perceptions of the roles of the great powers in Asia for the remainder of the 1970s.

One goal of the study is to evaluate Asian security preferences as seen by professionals from the region. The second is to assess the congruence between regional views of security requirements and some projected roles of the great powers in Asia. Only by juxtaposing the two can we discuss the likelihood of foreign policy cooperation or conflict between Asian nations and outside powers.

America's experience in Indochina over the past twenty years has demonstrated the limited applicability of conventional military force against a nonindustrialized peasant state in a war in which there are no front lines and in which the primary criterion of success is the allegiance and/or control of population rather than territory. The contrast between America's ability to preserve the status quo vis-à-vis the U.S.S.R. in the Cuban missile crisis or over Berlin with its inability to deal with North Vietnam is startling but not unlike the Soviets' inability to deal with Yugoslavia or Albania. Weak countries with a strong sense of national pride can make the use of force against themselves most unattractive, because their capacity for resistance makes the price of victory too high for the outsider.

America's future role in Asian security is ambiguous. Some combination of air, naval, and amphibious forces will probably remain in East Asia (Japan, the Republic of Korea, and the Philippines) through the remainder of the 1970s. Their purpose will be to serve as part of the global balance with the U.S.S.R., to deter direct or indirect Soviet intervention in local crises and, more importantly, to induce Soviet and Chinese cooperation in the peaceful solution of such crises if they arise. American security policy for the late 1970s must depend increasingly on a peaceful configuration of interests and power among local states rather than direct American intervention. U.S. diplomacy, then, must depend primarily on the instruments of trade, investment, and economic and military assistance.

For the remainder of non-Communist Asia, the lesson of Indochina is that future security arrangements must be indigenous and based on some combination of creating the domestic political and social conditions necessary to undermine any significant popular support for insurgencies and border-control operations with neighbors to insure that the availability of external sanctuaries is minimized. (Cooperation between Malaysia and Thailand and Malaysia and Indonesia are apt examples of the latter.)

As for the Vietnamese Communist victory itself, insofar as one American goal for involvement in Indochina in the beginning was to "contain" China, then having a strong satisfied Vietnamese-dominant Indochina on China's border might well effect a similar end. If so, then the bitterest irony of all is that America chose as its adversary the one Asian political movement which could best have achieved America's China containment policy. And now, when that policy has been superseded by détente and a new Asian configuration, the Indochinese Communists are in a position to help achieve a goal the United States has abandoned and the Soviet Union now pursues.

Most of the interviews granted by Asian officials carried the stipulation of anonymity, so I can only express my published appreciation in general terms. I am most grateful that so many foreign affairs officials were willing to take time away from very busy schedules to discuss their views of Asia's political future with a transient American scholar. Additional special thanks go to the numerous USIS cultural affairs officers who helped arrange these discussions and facilitated my travels through the region with my family. Finally, I owe particular thanks to Robert J. Pranger, AEI's director of foreign and defense policy studies, for his early encouragement of the project and his insightful discussion and helpful comments during its formulation.

Sheldon W. Simon
June 1975

ASIA and the PACIFIC

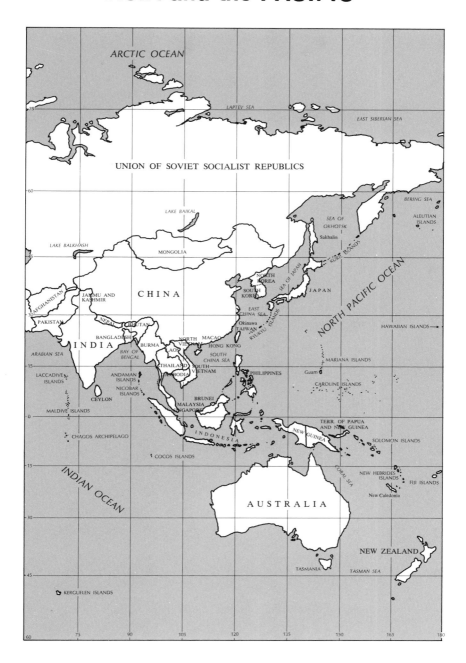

1
THE ASIAN FOREIGN POLICY ENVIRONMENT

From Alliance to Depolarization

Security is, to a large extent, a psychological state. Its presence or absence may prevail in a variety of institutional settings, from tight-knit alliance arrangements through collective defense pacts to pristine neutrality. There is no particular organizational framework which guarantees a country's security. In the long run international security depends on at least two national conditions: (1) a belief in the essential equity and justice of the international order, including the existence of acceptable mechanisms for change in that order; and (2) a belief that other states similarly perceive the international system at least to the extent that they will not choose to change its parameters by force.

Short of such widespread satisfaction with the international system, however, security in contemporary world politics has been sought mainly through military arrangements by two or more states for the purpose of either deterring a potential adversary or defending against it. This bias toward a military option in security thinking has created something of a self-fulfilling prophecy by contributing to a military view of international power and status (as distinct from, say, an economic view more open to Japan's role in world affairs) and to the competitive allocation of resources for weapons development and distribution. There, the paradox arises of ever-expanding military expenditures but no real increase in the level of international security, if by that phrase we mean an essential satisfaction with the international order and a belief that no significant powers are bent on changing that order by force.

The 1970s have witnessed increasing dissatisfaction with the post–World War II military approach to security in Asia. Although this discontent has not yet crystallized in an alternative security doctrine, there appears to be an emerging consensus that the defense arrangements of the past two decades are no longer applicable to the Asian realities of the mid-1970s. The search for new arrangements grows out of a perceived partial withdrawal of the Western states from their past military commitments, an emerging Western détente with both the U.S.S.R. and with China and the unsatisfactory denouement (from the non-Communist viewpoint) of the Indochina war which demonstrated the effective *political* limits of U.S. military power in defending an Asian ally. Perhaps even more to the point, the Vietnam War revealed how great power intervention in a protracted conflict can destroy a small power's society while attempting to save its government.

As middle and small powers, the Asian states are involved in rethinking their security interests and in disengaging themselves from what many of their leaders have come to view as potentially suffocating defense ties with outsiders.[1] As part of their reevaluation, many small powers have come to realize not only their limited capability to influence alliance policy with a great power but also that the great power's view of the alliance (as part of a global foreign policy posture) and the small power's view (total reliance for its national defense) were frequently incongruent if not incompatible.[2] A great power could vary its contribution to a regional alliance depending on other responsibilities. Thus, Singapore and Malaysia witnessed Britain's reduction of its contribution to their defense in the 1960s, growing out of London's adverse balance of payments and domestic economic difficulties.

Another liability incurred by a small power in an alliance with a large state is a loss of maneuverability, leading to a dependency relationship as distinct from a contributory one. In short, at least in security matters, the small state becomes an appendage of its larger protector, taking on the latter's conflicts as its own and seeing its own security priorities restructured if they do not fit into the great power's global posture.[3] American and North Vietnamese involvement in the

---

[1] There are exceptions to this generalization, particularly the Republic of Korea and to an extent, the Philippines and ostensibly nonaligned Singapore. Thailand, after Indochina's fall, is a special case. They will be discussed in later chapters.

[2] David Vital, *The Inequality of States* (London: Oxford University Press, 1967), pp. 29–30, and Robert Rothstein, *Alliances and Small Powers* (New York: Columbia University Press, 1968), p. 58.

[3] George Liska, *Alliance and the Third World*, International Affairs Study 5 (Washington, D.C.: Washington Center for Foreign Policy Research, Johns Hopkins University, 1968), p. 4. There have been cases in which this process is

Cambodian conflict since 1970 can be viewed in this context, since each outside adversary restructured the priorities of its Cambodian "ally" to further its own Indochina strategy.[4]

The global struggle for alignment in the two decades following World War II was pursued as a multiregional enterprise. Communist and Western powers contended for allegiance even among the ostensibly nonaligned so that they, too, by the mid-1960s, had moved toward a protector: Burma and Cambodia with China, India with both the United States and the Soviet Union ("double alignment"), and Indonesia at first with China and subsequently, after the 1965 abortive coup, with a regional organization—the Association of Southeast Asian Nations (ASEAN). These de facto alignments occurred because of a pervasive concern among the Asian states that some major power might try to establish regional hegemony, even though it is clear in retrospect that none had both the material capability and political intent.

Competitive alliance politics in Asia began with the U.S. containment policy, initiated by Secretary of State Dean Acheson's January 1950 address to the National Press Club in Washington. The speech delineated the American defense perimeter desired at that time by the Joint Chiefs of Staff and General Douglas MacArthur, which excluded Korea—a decision which would soon be regretted.[5]

Moscow had, in rapid succession, consolidated its hold on Eastern Europe, probed for weak spots in Iran, Turkey, and Greece, launched the Berlin blockade, and exploded its first atomic bomb. Turning to Asia, the Cominform encouraged insurrection in the Philippines, Burma, India, Indonesia, and Malaya. Mao Tse-tung's victory on the China mainland extended Soviet power across the Eurasian land mass. And in that context, Stalin backed the North Korean use of force to add the Korean peninsula, directly confronting U.S. military personnel for the first time. Thus, President Truman decided to meet force with force, extending the European containment concept to Asia. Within five years, defense treaties were signed with Japan, South Korea, the Republic of China on Taiwan, the Philippines, Australia and New Zealand. The creation of an additional eight-nation Southeast Asia

---

reversed, however, and small states have used great power military assistance for their own purposes. A classic example would be the American provision of military equipment to Pakistan in the 1950s and 1960s, employed by the latter against India rather than as part of the American containment policy.

[4] See Sheldon W. Simon, *War and Politics in Cambodia: A Communications Analysis* (Durham: Duke University Press, 1974), passim.

[5] Dean Acheson, *Present at the Creation: My Years in the State Department* (New York: W. W. Norton, 1969), pp. 355–358.

Treaty Organization (SEATO) added Thailand and Pakistan to the list of Asian states to which the United States attached security importance. SEATO was buttressed by a separate protocol which seemed to extend its protection to the nonmember states of South Vietnam, Laos, and Cambodia, should they request it. Permanent U.S. forces were deployed from a growing base complex in Japan, Okinawa, the Philippines, South Korea, Taiwan, Guam, and later in the course of the Vietnam War, South Vietnam and Thailand.

The fallacy in this policy, as in many politico-military postures, is that it was designed to protect against or deter the situation which had precipitated it rather than those which might follow. It was thought, with justification, that the North Koreans would not have invaded the South had they expected to meet American forces. Thus, a policy which would serve well to deter an overt, conventional attack on South Korea was expanded to cover much of both island and mainland Asia without taking into account the individual political-military situations in each state or the varying U.S. interests in maintaining the status quo.[6] The containment posture reached its nadir, of course, when the threat became a combination of external infiltration and support and internal revolt, instead of overt attack.

The American alliance system in Asia served an additional purpose to the provision of base facilities for U.S. troops and equipment cited above. It legitimized U.S. intervention in Vietnam as a SEATO protocol state and provided the rationale for involvement in the domestic politics of the latter in hopes of strengthening its internal order. Not only was the effort ultimately fruitless but also the United States was unable to involve other SEATO members effectively in its Vietnam policy. Indeed, the only American allies to contribute significantly to the war were South Korea and Thailand. The former participated for a variety of motives, including the promise of modern military equipment from the United States, the desire to demonstrate its reliability so that the Americans would not reduce their commitment to the R.O.K., and a genuine belief that Communist aggression should be resisted wherever it occurred.[7] The latter also benefited from increased military support but had the additional desire to demonstrate forcefully their antipathy over a Communist-controlled Indochina to the Vietnamese Communists.

---

6 See the very perceptive discussion in Ralph N. Clough, "East Asia," in Henry Owen, ed., *The Next Phase in Foreign Policy* (Washington, D.C.: The Brookings Institution, 1973), pp. 49–51. See also Robert J. Pranger, *Defense Implications of International Indeterminacy* (Washington, D.C.: American Enterprise Institute, 1972), pp. 6–10.

7 Author's interviews in Seoul, May 1973.

SEATO's history typified America's Asian alliance problems in the 1960s and revealed the narrow parameters of multilateral military action against Communist-inspired united front insurgencies. The organization was never meant to be a strong collective defense arrangement. Motives for participation varied with each actor. For the United States it became a means of legitimizing overseas bases and deployment as well as military intervention when Washington so chose. (It did not so choose in Laos in 1962 but did in Vietnam three years later.) For Australia, New Zealand, and Great Britain, SEATO was a device to sustain an ongoing U.S. commitment to Southeast Asia, protecting the northern flank of Malaya at a time when the British were contemplating their own withdrawal. For Pakistan, it served as a means to obtain U.S. military aid against India, just as had its adherence to the Baghdad Pact (subsequently CENTO).

The only country in the region directly benefiting from SEATO's security role was Thailand. Since the American commitment to the organization was to keep communism north of the seventeenth parallel, the Thais would be the direct beneficiaries of its success or the probable future frontline should it fail. Thailand's skepticism over SEATO's efficacy was manifest in Foreign Minister Thanat's insistence that the United States initial a separate bilateral guarantee to Thailand that its defense was important regardless of SEATO activities. The ensuing Rusk-Thanat memorandum (1962) directly followed the organization's unwillingness to become involved in the Laotian civil war.

Indeed, some analysts have argued that SEATO was not only ineffective as a multilateral defense arrangement (as distinct from an institutionalized rationale for a permanent U.S. military presence in the region) but that, in fact, it was provocative. Those states adhering to the organization became targets for insurgent subversion both to weaken the American position and to demonstrate the treaty's ineffectuality.[8]

SEATO, although the most prominent, was not the only Western defense arrangement whose utility was being questioned in the wake of U.S. military involvement in Indochina. The parallel Anglo-Malaysian Defense Agreement for the protection of Malaysia and Singapore came to an end on 31 October 1971. It had proved quite effective against Sukarno's confrontation in the mid-1960s. But with the demise of an Indonesian threat, Great Britain's domestic economic difficulties led to a decision to draw down its forces east of Suez to a series of token contingents. The new Five Power Defense

---

[8] See, for example, Liska, *Alliance and the Third World*, pp. 36–37.

Agreement came into operation on 1 November, including Australian and New Zealand forces. The agreement, however, much like SEATO, calls only for joint consultation in the event of a security threat. Moreover, with the 1973 advent of a Labour government in Canberra, even Australia's minimal commitment to Malaysia and Singapore was slated to be terminated by the middle of the decade, although New Zealand stated its contingent would remain as long as the Malaysians desired it. ANZUK forces were particularly helpful in providing the training necessary to give Malaysia and Singapore an air and naval reconnaissance capability. And the two neighbors still maintain a joint air defense system even though most other political and economic ties have been severed.[9]

Thus by the early 1970s, the Southeast Asian political environment was depolarizing: the British had greatly reduced their military presence in the Five Power Defense Agreement; the United States was disengaging its troops from Vietnam and reducing its total forces in Asia to the pre-Vietnam War level; China had embarked on a major new program of people-to-people and state-to-state diplomacy for the first time since the mid-1950s; and the Soviet Union was increasing its commercial and diplomatic ties to the region. The Asian states themselves were preparing to look more within themselves and to each other for solutions to domestic and regional security problems. A key question confronting them all concerned the new role the United States would write for itself in a depolarized Asian setting. Put somewhat differently, what was the meaning of the Nixon Doctrine for Asian security planning?

The Nixon Doctrine and Ambiguity in America's Asian Commitments

Much has been written about the Nixon Doctrine since then President Nixon enunciated his post-Vietnam War scenario on Guam in July 1969. Many of the interpretations of the administration's purpose have been contradictory, yet still plausible, because they have been based on differing premises. Some analysts, such as Melvin Gurtov and Earl Ravenal, view the doctrine as an attempt to sustain an American forward defense posture in Asia at a political and economic price acceptable to the U.S. Congress and the American public. Others,

---

[9] For a discussion of the Anglo-Malaysian Defense Agreement and the successor Five Power Agreement, see T. B. Millar, "Prospects for Regional Security Cooperation in Southeast Asia," in R. S. Milne and Mark Zacher, eds., *Conflict and Stability in Southeast Asia* (New York: Doubleday-Anchor, 1974).

like Robert Osgood, see the doctrine as the first step in a new American policy of sophisticated "balance of presence" diplomacy which will reduce regional tensions and shift the discourse of great power competition from military to economic influence.[10] At this point in history, there is no definitive explanation or prediction of U.S. security policy toward Asia because both America and Asia are still engaged in a process of transition. The Indochina war has only recently terminated, and the American alliance structure remains at least formally intact. Nevertheless, Asian states are making plans for an environment quite different from the one they have known for the last twenty-five to thirty years.

Perhaps the best way to understand the Nixon Doctrine is to examine its most prominent interpretations and relate them to probable concerns of Asian leaders. As Robert Pranger points out, the need for a new conception of American security interests toward the third world grew out of the unsatisfactory limited war strategy of the 1960s under which any insurgency openly supported by Communist propaganda or supplies, regardless of location, was viewed as a challenge to America's safety and elicited some kind of response from Washington. Although many of these local wars could be interpreted by traditional international law as acts of aggression, they were politically popular both within the societies in which they were fought and with international public opinion because they were conducted in the name of a universal principle: freedom from oppression. The United States placed itself in the anomalous position of frequently backing unpopular repressive regimes against politico-military "liberation movements" which publicly expressed the same value to which the United States itself was said to be committed—*national liberation*. Thus, one goal of the Nixon Doctrine was to divorce the United States from a policy of automatically backing illegitimate regimes against political foes who may have some Communist support.[11]

However, such a change could not come about abruptly, without the risk of undermining the security plans of a number of Asian states. Therefore, one of the first clarifications of the doctrine was

---

[10] See Melvin Gurtov, "Security by Proxy: The Nixon Doctrine and Southeast Asia," in Milne and Zacher, *Conflict and Stability in Southeast Asia;* and Earl Ravenal, "The Nixon Doctrine and Our Asian Commitments," *Foreign Affairs,* vol. 42, no. 2 (January 1971). For an alternative interpretation, see Robert E. Osgood, "The Nixon Doctrine and Strategy," in Robert Osgood et al., *Retreat from Empire? The First Nixon Administration* (Baltimore: The Johns Hopkins Press, 1973).

[11] Pranger, *Defense Implications,* p. 10.

an attempt to reassure U.S. allies that (1) all treaty commitments would be maintained, that is, not unilaterally abrogated by the United States; (2) a nuclear shield against a nuclear threat would be provided for U.S. allies and for other states deemed essential for American security (although no criteria were outlined to determine which states fell into the latter category); and (3) in the case of other types of aggression, the United States would furnish military and economic assistance in accordance with its treaty commitments. Two changes from previous U.S. policies were implicit in this last point: (1) the most obvious was the decoupling of an American force response from conventional, local aggression; (2) a more subtle but perhaps even more important change was the decision not to specify insurgency as a subtype of aggression, thus permitting Washington the option of not becoming involved in future insurgent wars which appeared to be essentially internally generated. As Nixon put it in his 1970 "state of the world" message:

> It is misleading . . . to pose the fundamental question so largely in terms of commitments . . . We are not involved in the world because we have commitments; we have commitments because we are involved. Our interests must shape our commitments, rather than the other way around.[12]

What the President seemed to be saying was that America's commitments would be reevaluated (and perhaps altered) in the light of its negative Vietnam experience and its new global relations with China and the Soviet Union. Asia would no longer remain the primary region of U.S. global concern as it was in the 1960s. Upon the conclusion of hostilities in Indochina, there would be neither military nor economic cause for it to remain so. This was not to say, however, that Asia would be written off as an important theater of American operations and influence. The issue was one of degree and style rather than the abnegation of America's political and economic presence. Influence and access would be substituted for residence and control. And the U.S. military presence in Asia would become intermittent and dependent on mutually agreed specific security threats rather than permanent and a target for nationalist opprobrium.

A demonstration of the kind of military force the United States would employ in future Asian conflicts occurred with the spring and December 1972 naval and aerial raids over Hanoi and Haiphong

---

[12] Cited in Alan M. Jones, Jr., "Nixon and the World," in Alan M. Jones, ed., *U.S. Foreign Policy in a Changing World* (New York: David McKay, 1973), p. 25.

as well as the extensive American bombing of Khmer Rouge and North Vietnamese forces in Cambodia through mid-August 1973. Leaving aside their military efficacy, which appeared to be considerable in North Vietnam and negligible in Cambodia, these tactics proved to be clearly acceptable to American public opinion, which raised virtually no protest despite the fact that some of the heaviest bombing in the whole eight years of the U.S. military involvement in Indochina had occurred.[13] What this suggests is not that the American public desires a global withdrawal but that future U.S. global policies should be pursued at a lower cost in American (though not necessarily Asian) lives.

Critics of the Nixon Doctrine, such as Ravenal, Gurtov, and Jones cited above, argue, however, that the United States is neither changing its commitments in Asia nor its view of communism as expansionist. Washington is searching instead for a military posture which is more acceptable domestically but is still designed to counter Asian Communist insurgencies by military force. The only difference between this policy and that of the Johnson administration is that the United States will possess a smaller repertoire of tactics to employ and will maintain a smaller number of forces on station in Asia. Such a posture, according to these critics, is highly provocative because it encourages American military and political planners to compensate for a lack of conventional force through the planned use of tactical nuclear weapons (à la NATO); or, alternatively, because of a reduced military capability but no change in defense commitments, both the United States and its allies increase their risk of military stalemate or defeat.[14] Two underlying premises shared by these critics are that the primary challenge to Asian stability will continue to be externally backed Communist insurgencies and that the United States will continue to respond militarily to such challenges.

There is a different conception of the Nixon Doctrine, however, still in the process of being articulated, which is more complex than the dominant view of the critics summarized above. This view begins with the premise of a depolarizing Asia in which both new problems and opportunities present themselves to the region's leaders. Because the United States has already begun to deal directly with China and the Soviet Union, traditional anticommunism can no longer be the

---

[13] See the discussion of public opinion poll data on the spring 1972 bombing of North Vietnam in Robert W. Tucker, "The American Outlook: Change and Continuity," in Osgood et al., *Retreat from Empire?* pp. 29–78.

[14] In addition to the sources in footnote nine, p. 6, see also the Ravenal and Gelb chapters in Earl C. Ravenal, ed., *Peace with China? U.S. Decisions for Asia* (New York: Liveright Press, 1971), pp. 21–48.

guiding principle of U.S.-Asian policy. A diminished anticommunism implies a reduced need for U.S. intervention, thus justifying the intermittent access concept presented above. In short, the Nixon Doctrine may be viewed as the tentative first step toward a détente relationship with the adversaries of the past twenty-five to thirty years, while at the same time providing interim protection for U.S. allies and a way of maintaining global influence as a great power.

There are several implications of this view of the Nixon Doctrine which portend significant changes for Asian international politics. The American decision to deal directly with its adversaries reduces the importance of ally relationships. Indeed, a reduction in the intensity of these relationships may even serve as an inducement for adversaries to enter into new, limited, cooperative endeavors. One way of interpreting the clause renouncing any interest in regional hegemony in the February 1972 Nixon-Chou En-lai Shanghai communiqué is that it contained an American assurance to China that the United States was not engaged in establishing a permanent political sphere of influence in Asia—the ultimate American hope being that China would be encouraged by this attestation to moderate its own policies and develop a stake in preserving the current international structure. China would, in effect, be enlisted as a partner in a reformulated containment policy, insofar as *containment* meant a preservation of the integrity of the Asian states' system.[15]

If the Nixon Doctrine is America's first step on the road to regional détente, new pitfalls will confront the maintenance of American influence in Asia. Whereas in the past two decades the United States preserved regional dominance through political, military, and economic aid programs designed to protect new states against supposed Communist predators, both the rationale for these programs and the region's willingness to accept them may now be undermined. There will be little incentive to accept American views of Asian security—a situation inherent in the Nixon administration's call for a regional balance of power in Asia—as the region's leaders observe the United States disengaging militarily and reducing its economic support. The U.S. administration's one and one-half war defense preparedness doctrine has already formalized the diminished importance of Asia for American security planning. Where the number of American troops in Europe has remained constant, all garrisons in Asia have been cut back to the point that virtually no ground force capability remains. This absence of ground-force capability clearly

---

[15] For an insightful discussion of this seeming paradox, see Tucker, "American Outlook," p. 55.

underscores the second of the Nixon Doctrine's injunctions against U.S. involvement in future land wars on the Asian continent. American military forces in Asia by the mid-1970s, then, were confined to air and naval arms, which provided a support and interdiction capacity but not the ability to take and hold territory.

In sum, the Nixon Doctrine, incorporated now by the Ford administration, searches for stability through détente rather than confrontation. Explanations for this change in orientation include new priorities in U.S. domestic programs, the unsatisfactory experience in Indochina, an American realization that economic assistance was a panacea neither for democracy nor economic growth, and a downgrading of the threat of Communist aggression through the facile metaphor of falling dominoes. But any success the Nixon Doctrine has attained to date must be attributed as much to Sino-Soviet antipathy as to U.S. policy alterations. The Sino-Soviet split has been a primary incentive for both Communist great powers to improve their relations with the United States and reduce their level of conflict support against Asian non-Communist governments.

The New Soviet Presence

Both domestic and international factors account for the dramatic diplomatic, commercial, and to a smaller extent, military increase in the Soviet Asian presence since the beginning of the 1970s. (These will be discussed in detail in Chapter 3.) The United States has viewed increased Russian diplomatic activity in virtually all Asian states, as well as the development of a special relationship with India and Bangladesh as a result of the latter's war of independence, with equanimity. As Soviet commitments and influence expanded, it was believed the U.S.S.R. would encounter constraints similar to those experienced by the United States. The ensuing frustrations would render the Russians more willing to moderate their competition with the United States and even cooperate in decoupling third world activities from more crucial Soviet-American bilateral relationships.[16] The fact that the intensive bombing of Hanoi/Haiphong in the spring of 1972 did not lead to a Soviet postponement of the Nixon summit visit provided some evidence for the hypothesis that the U.S.S.R. placed higher priority on détente with the United States than on facilitating the politico-military goals of a recalcitrant Asian ally. It appears that the Nixon administration's hope for mutual restraint has been compatible with Soviet aims since that time. A détente

---

[16] Osgood, "Nixon Doctrine and Strategy," p. 12.

fits into Soviet plans of stabilizing its European front in order to cope with China, relaxing tension with the United States in order to create division within U.S. alliances, and seeking U.S. technology to help repair its ailing economy.

The Soviets have been suspicious of third world revolutionary movements for some time, finding them unpredictable, difficult to control, and oriented more toward Maoist, peasant, organizational style than toward the Soviet, clandestine, cellular structure. As early as the mid-1950s, Russian ideologues rationalized a preference for dealing with third world governments rather than Communist parties by referring to those with an anticapitalist bent as "national democracies" and viewing them as having set foot on the path to socialist development. Sukarno's fall in Indonesia in the mid-1960s proved a kind of watershed for Soviet policy toward Asian radical nationalists, as Moscow watched its carefully cultivated position destroyed along with "Bung Karno." Since then, the U.S.S.R. has dealt with Asian governments regardless of their ties to the West and has established commercial or diplomatic ties with such staunch anti-Communist and private-enterprise bastions as Thailand, the Philippines, and Malaysia/Singapore.

Although the Russians appear to have lost interest in revolution, there has been an upswing in their desire to achieve equality with the United States as a great power in military affairs. Some analysts attribute the recent Soviet building of general purpose forces to a way of compensating for the lack of attraction of its economic system. Where the rule of bureaucratic conservatives has resulted in a loss of economic innovation and an inability to meet growing Russian consumer demands, the leadership has turned to building its military capacity as an alternative means of claiming superpower status.[17] There is an irony involved in this Soviet emphasis on military capacity as an index of national achievement, for it occurs at a time when the general international system seems to be turning away from traditional military status competition and moving toward a status based on the possession of economic resources and technological development for general welfare. The Soviets are aware of the disparity between their high military position and relatively low economic status, and Secretary Brezhnev has apparently staked a good portion of his future political career on overcoming Russian economic deficits through the importation of Western technology.

---

[17] Representative of this view are Zbigniew Brezinski, "U.S.-Soviet Relations," in Owen, ed., *The Next Phase*, and Herbert Dinerstern, "The Soviet Outlook: America, Europe, and China," in Osgood et al., *Retreat From Empire?* p. 116.

On the other hand, the North Vietnamese/Viet Cong victory in the spring of 1975 was accomplished through massive Soviet military assistance.

Nevertheless, the U.S.S.R. appears to be following contradictory principles: on the one hand it is attempting to husband its own resources and import more from abroad, while on the other, it is dissipating resources by supplying such costly and demanding clients as Egypt, Syria, and India. None of these countries can be considered as *loyalist* to the U.S.S.R.; the relationship is pragmatic rather than one of sentiment. And as events in Egypt since 1973 demonstrated, a middle power can disengage from the Soviet relationship with relative impunity so long as alternative suppliers for its military and economic needs exist. Again as Egypt showed, the alternative suppliers need not be great powers. In Cairo's case, of course, they were oil-rich Arab neighbors.

The Soviet relationship with India, however, proved more troublesome than its Egyptian counterpart, largely because New Delhi possessed no alternative allies. Soviet military support and the promise of diversionary action on China's border, should that be necessary, provided India with the military confidence it needed to change the political structure of the subcontinent.[18] India's successful politico-military gambit, however, was contrary to America's conception of a common Soviet-American interest in preventing military changes in the status quo which the U.S. President and his chief foreign policy advisor deemed essential if the Nixon Doctrine was to work effectively. As a direct response to the Bangladesh War, Nixon admonished the Soviets in his 1972 world report:

> The Soviet Union in the 1970's is projecting a political and military presence without precedent in many new regions of the globe. Over the past three years, we have sought to encourage constructive trends in U.S.-Soviet relations. It would be dangerous to world peace if our efforts to promote a detente between the super powers were interpreted as an opportunity for the strategic expansion of Soviet power. If we failed to take a stand, such an interpretation could only have been encouraged, and the genuine relaxation of tensions we have been seeking could have been jeopardized.[19]

The President was referring in large part to the growing complement of the Soviet Pacific fleet in the Indian Ocean where its

---

[18] See Wayne Wilcox, *The Emergence of Bangladesh: Problems and Opportunities for a Redefined American Policy in South Asia* (Washington, D.C.: American Enterprise Institute, 1973), pp. 45–46.

[19] Cited in Jones, "Nixon and the World," p. 59.

ship-operating days increased from 1800 in 1968 to 8800 in 1972, although much of the latter was accounted for by crisis deployment during the Bangladesh War and the activities of auxiliary vessels in the clearing of Dacca and Chittagong ports.[20] There were reports of a permanent Soviet naval presence in these ports. The fact that the clearing and salvage operation was commanded by a Soviet admiral lent some credence to the belief that the Russian interest in the Bangladesh ports was more than altruistic.[21] Although the Russians have no active combat troops on the Indian Ocean, their force there is believed to include one large destroyer, one escort, two mine-sweepers, a submarine, and ten support ships, not counting the ships engaged in cleaning Chittagong. By contrast, in mid-1974 the United States maintained only a single amphibious command ship and two destroyers in the area, supplemented from time to time with carrier task forces from the Seventh Fleet.[22]

The significance of a Soviet military naval presence is not so much its capacity to employ force but rather its political mission. The fleet's movement signals intentions to friend and foe alike and causes the latter to risk conflict if it wishes to intervene in a third country against the former's desires. Just as the Mediterranean was no longer a Western lake after the Soviets obtained port facilities in Egypt in the mid to late 1960s, so the Indian Ocean also is no longer a Western preserve. Thus, the American attempt to demonstrate its military muscle in December 1971 during the Bangladesh War by moving a carrier task force off the coast of Bengal was neutralized by the fact that a Soviet contingent followed close behind. In effect the presence of both fleets in the Indian Ocean probably means an end to gunboat diplomacy, since neither can provide a credible threat of naval intervention in a local conflict *if* such intervention is opposed by the other. A salutory implication of this standoff is that it will tend to prevent local conflicts from being sucked into global politics.[23]

Mixed Signals from Peking

State-to-State Relations. In addition to its conflict with the Soviet Union, the most important external factor responsible for the People's

---

[20] See the very perceptive essay by Barry M. Blechman, *The Changing Soviet Navy* (Washington, D.C.: The Brookings Institution, 1973), p. 13. Much of the ensuing discussion on Soviet naval affairs is drawn from this study.

[21] See the report in the *Far Eastern Economic Review*, 4 February 1974, p. 20.

[22] Bernard Weintraub, "The Value of Diego Garcia," *The New York Times*, 2 June 1974.

[23] The Soviet position in relation to Asian neutralism is discussed in Chapter 3.

14

Republic of China's (P.R.C.) post–Cultural Revolution opening to world politics and government-to-government relations has been the reduction of America's military posture in Asia. As Doak Barnett points out, American signals to Peking began to change as early as 1962, when Washington refused to support a Chinese Nationalist threat to reconquer the mainland. Even in the course of the Vietnam War, which witnessed a hardening of postures in both capitals, the United States reassured China that it had no designs on North Vietnam—a communication reciprocated by Mao in his 1965 interview with Edgar Snow, promising no direct Chinese intervention in the war so long as the integrity of the D.R.V. was not threatened. By 1970 the Seventh Fleet had stopped patrolling the Straits of Taiwan; Okinawa's reversion to Japan in 1972 meant its denuclearization; and after the January 1973 Paris accord, despite the continuation of the Indochina war, U.S. forces in Southeast Asia, Japan, and Korea were reduced in number. All of these moves were encapsulated in the Nixon Doctrine's downgrading of any Chinese military threat to its neighbors.[24] Thus, as James Thomson put it, foreign policy cycles in Washington and Peking have finally coincided for the first time since 1949, permitting pragmatic cooperation because both desire a political-military equilibrium in the Asian-Pacific region, since each lacks either the capacity or the will to drive for regional hegemony.[25] While China approves the reduction of the U.S. military posture in Asia, it has indicated on several occasions that it does not wish to see a complete American withdrawal. China's interest in an American détente is premised on the maintenance of U.S. Asian involvement as an element in the regional politico-military mix of forces.

On the level of state-to-state diplomacy, Peking has started a campaign to reassure third-world states (a category which includes virtually all of its Asian neighbors) of its benign intentions and political support in such multilateral forums as the United Nations. In a series of addresses at the UN, China's representatives enunciated their country's principles on aid, both revealing its policy on dealing with the third world and differentiating it from those of the major industrial states. According to Peking: (1) all trade recipients should be treated as diplomatic equals, (2) there should be no strings attached to aid of either a political or an economic character, (3) the purpose

---

[24] A. Doak Barnett, "U.S. Relations with China," in Owen, ed., *The Next Phase*, p. 147.

[25] James C. Thomson, Jr., "The United States and China in the Seventies," in John H. Gilbert, ed., *The New Era in American Foreign Policy* (New York: St. Martin's, 1973). See also, Robert Scalapino, "China and the Balance of Power," *Foreign Affairs*, January 1974.

of aid should be self-liquidating, that is, it should facilitate the recipient country's becoming ultimately independent of the aid, (4) there should be either no interest charge or only a nominal service fee for the aid, and (5) aid requirements should be determined by the recipients' needs rather than the political or economic goals of the donor.[26] Such charitable principles reflect the fact, of course, that China is not a major donor (although it has equalled or surpassed the Soviet Union in recent years in some categories) and that it is better able to place political considerations—in this case the projection of a helpful mien—well ahead of economic return on investment. Generous Chinese credit terms also permit Peking to point a reproving finger at the superpowers who are accused of "neocolonialist economic plunder." The U.S.S.R. has become the particular target of such opprobrium. In the United Nations, Vice Premier Teng Hsiao-ping summarized the Chinese bill of particulars against alleged Soviet exploitation of the third world in the following manner:

> Its usual practice is to tag a high price on outmoded equipment and substandard weapons and exchange them for strategic raw materials and farm produce of the developing countries. Selling arms and ammunition in a big way, it has become an international merchant of death. It often takes advantage of others' difficulties to press for the repayment of debts. In the recent Middle East war, it bought Arab oil at a low price with the large amount of foreign exchange it had earned by peddling munitions, and then sold it at a high price, making staggering profits in the twinkle of an eye. Moreover, it preaches the theory of "limited sovereignty," alleges that the resources of developing countries are international property, and even asserts that "the sovereignty over the natural resources depends to a great extent upon the capability of utilizing these resources by the industry of the developing countries." These are out-and-out imperialist fallacies. . . . A socialist country that is true to its name ought to . . . render support and assistance to oppressed countries and nations and help them develop their national economy. But this superpower is doing exactly the opposite. This is additional proof that it is socialism in words and imperialism in deeds.[27]

It matters less that these charges are composed of half-truths and some outright falsehoods than that they accurately depict that

[26] *Peking Review*, nos. 17 and 28, 28 April and 14 July 1972.
[27] Address by Teng Hsiao-ping to the special session of the UN General Assembly on Energy and the Developing Areas, New China News Agency (NCNA), 10 April 1974.

segment of China's conflict with the U.S.S.R. over influence among developing states, with China urging the latter to sever economic ties that could lead to political clientage. The Soviets have naturally refuted these Chinese recriminations in their own propaganda and have gone on to insist that there is no basis for China's recalcitrance, that contrary to Chinese accusations, the U.S.S.R. has neither territorial nor economic claims on Peking, and that Moscow has repeatedly offered to conclude a nonaggression pact with Peking since January 1971 to no avail.[28]

Clearly a prime motivating factor in China's improved state-to-state relations since 1971 has been its concern over potential self-induced isolation while the U.S.S.R. has been engaging in a forward Asian diplomacy. Thus, the 1970s have witnessed both China and the Soviet Union vigorously promoting their respective positions in Asia in hopes of diminishing the other's success.

The Asian states themselves initially reacted cautiously to both Chinese and Soviet "smiling face" diplomacy. Indeed, the November 1971 bloodless coup in Thailand, perpetrated by Premier Thanom, occurred in part to decelerate what was viewed as a too precipitous regional reorientation toward Peking. Thai leaders, along with those of Indonesia, the Philippines, and Malaysia were concerned over the allegiance of their Chinese citizens in the event of a new strong P.R.C. position in Asia. Through 1971, ASEAN members insisted that diplomatic relations could only follow firm guarantees that Peking would cease support for Maoist insurgencies in their territories. During the same period, the Philippines moved to ease its citizenship requirements for local Chinese in hopes of assimilating them.[29]

Indonesia insisted that diplomatic ties could recur only if Peking cut off support for the Kalimantan rebels, ejected exiled PKI leaders from China, and halted radio propaganda against the Suharto government. By 1973, the last demand had virtually been met, and China had invited an Indonesian ping pong team to Peking. Although the invitation was declined, Indonesian athletes did participate with their Chinese counterparts in Thailand in the spring of 1974. Indonesian officials, however, cautioned the international press against making too much of the athletic contest by going beyond sports to diplomacy. Nevertheless, Jakarta's reticence in reestablishing official

---

[28] Brezhnev's Report on the occasion of the 50th Anniversary of the U.S.S.R., Tass, 21 December 1973.

[29] R. S. Milne, "The Influence on Foreign Policy of Ethnic Minorities with External Ties," in Milne and Zacher, eds., Conflict and Stability, pp. 105–106.

contacts with Peking probably has more to do with its concern over the loyalty of its three million Chinese than with any real worry over new Communist uprisings. Foreign ministry officials have admitted as much on more than one occasion. And P.R.C. officials have assured Indonesia privately that they would not support new Communist insurgencies.[30]

In the Philippines, President Marcos sent his brother-in-law as an unofficial emissary to Peking, while his wife visited Moscow. Chinese officials expressed an interest in trade ties and assured Filipino journalists against any exportation of revolution.[31] Moreover, Mrs. Marcos herself visited Peking for National Day celebrations on 1 October 1974, managing to conclude a trade contract for petroleum supplies to the Philippines in the course of her visit. Diplomatic relations with the P.R.C. will probably be established sometime in 1975.

Of the five ASEAN states, only one—Malaysia—had actually opened diplomatic relations by mid-1974. Kuala Lumpur had established three conditions for the normalization of relations: (1) Peking must withdraw support from the Malayan Communist party (MCP) which was operating on both the Thai border and in Sarawak, (2) it must stop the broadcasts of the MCP radio located in China's Yunnan province, and (3) it must clearly indicate that the overseas Chinese are subject solely to the laws of their country of residence.[32] And China appears to have made some tacit concessions to Malaysian demands. Chou En-lai has indicated to visiting Southeast Asian leaders that Peking is prepared to accept jus soli for those Chinese who have acquired local citizenship. This position is comparable to that agreed to by Peking in its treaty with Indonesia over a decade ago. Yet the P.R.C. appears to be unwilling to renounce protection of some 200,000 Chinese in Malaysia who have not acquired citizenship.[33] Moreover, there is no evidence that an agreement has been reached on the cessation of MCP broadcasts or Chinese aid to the insurgent party. These are difficult requests for Peking to comply with because they go beyond bilateral relations and involve Peking's claim to leadership among socialist-revolutionary movements vis-à-

---

[30] Agence France Presse (AFP), 31 December 1973, and Jakarta Domestic Service in Indonesian, 2 March 1974.

[31] A useful summary of Chinese-Southeast Asian diplomatic probings in the early 1970s may be found in Frank C. Langdon, "China's Policy in Southeast Asia," in Milne and Zacher, eds., *Conflict and Stability*, pp. 320–323.

[32] Stephen Chee, "Malaysia and Singapore: The Political Economy of Multiracial Development," *Asian Survey*, vol. 14, no. 2 (February 1974), p. 188.

[33] Ibid.

vis the U.S.S.R.[34] They are, then, both a part of the Sino-Soviet conflict as well as an element of political influence in bilateral dealings with the governments of non-Communist Southeast Asia.

From the time of the student revolt in October 1973, Thailand's new government has joined the regional trend exploring the possibility of better relations with the P.R.C. Following Peking's diplomatic style of beginning with people-to-people relations and then moving up to formal governmental contacts, Thailand has exchanged a number of athletic delegations in the last two years, invariably led by high-level political officials. In the course of these dialogues it was established that Peking did not view the presence of U.S. troops and bases as an obstacle to better bilateral relations. By late 1973, the P.R.C. had followed its initial sports activities with an offer to sell crude oil to Thailand and a promise to stop offensive radio broadcasts.[35] In 1974, Thailand's National Assembly had debated the wisdom of revoking the prohibition against commercial relations with Peking. The only real obstacles to a lifting of the ban appeared to be concern that no single group of Thais reap inordinate benefits from a new trade relationship and that no sector of the Thai domestic economy be threatened by low-cost Chinese imports. Significantly, the only objections to trade ties were economic rather than political. And in February 1974 Chou En-lai told Thai Defense Minister Thawi Chunlasap that Peking would cut support for Thai insurgents it had been aiding for the past ten years.[36]

Relations with Regional Insurgents. Several careful observers of China's foreign policy have noted that Peking's aid to Asian insurgent movements is orchestrated to reflect the character of its relations with non-Communist Asian governments; for instance, amicable governmental ties tend to be reciprocated by a reduction of Chinese material and propaganda support to insurgents. The obverse also holds, of course.[37] Thus, for example, it has been demonstrated that large-scale Chinese support for the relatively small Thai Communist

---

[34] China's general attitude toward and relations with insurgent movements is discussed below.

[35] See the "China '73 Focus" of the *Far Eastern Economic Review*, 1 October 1973, p. 38. See also Bangkok Domestic Service in Thai, 27 August and 26 October 1973, *The Nation*, 8 November 1973, and the *Bangkok Post*, 29 December 1973.

[36] *The Nation*, 17 February 1974, and the *New York Times*, 17 February 1974.

[37] See particularly Melvin Gurtov, *China and Southeast Asia: The Politics of Survival* (Lexington, Mass.: D.C. Heath, 1971); and Peter Van Ness, *Revolution in Chinese Foreign Policy: Peking's Support for Wars of National Liberation* (Berkeley: University of California Press, 1970).

party insurgency in the North began only after the Tonkin Gulf incident and American bombing of the Ho Chi Minh Trail had led to the involvement of Thai personnel and Thai bases in the Vietnam War.[38]

The nature of Chinese support for regional insurgents was held at a low enough level not to elicit any major American reaction. It consisted of asylum for insurgent leaders on the run, propaganda facilities, and training and military support, but *not* Chinese personnel (with the infrequent exception of some advisors or observers). The modest character of China's support for Asian insurgents indicated that Peking was not so committed to insurgent success that its support could not be reversed with appropriate changes in political behavior on the part of the host country. It also reflected the fact that there were fairly stringent geographical limits to China's extension of *continuous* support, confining it primarily to the belt of hill-tribe and border areas in Indochina, Burma, and Thailand, with virtually no such support in the lower-mainland or archipelago regions of Southeast Asia.

Regional leaders are cognizant of the broader political meaning of Peking's ties to the insurgents and hope that many of their security problems will diminish if they can effect a rapprochement with the P.R.C. Thus, Thanat Khoman, an advisor to former Thai Prime Minister Sanya, though not an "insider" in Thai foreign policy circles, stated:

> We have seen examples in certain countries like Burma and Ceylon, that if you reach understanding with the sources of support for insurgency or for communist illegal activities, then the illegal activities stopped. The case of Burma is very convincing. At a certain moment the communist activities supported by China were quite apparent in Burma, but after General Ne Win went to Peking (1972) those activities have ceased or have been reduced to a great extent.[39]

As state-to-state relations improve, Peking faces a risk in diminishing its support for regional insurgencies if the insurgents possess both an indigenous base and an alternative source of external support. There have been some reports of a disenchantment with Peking on the part of the Thai Communist party and the possibility of its turning more to Hanoi for aid. Professional observers generally acknowledge two separate insurgencies in north and northeast

---

[38] Daniel Lovelace, *China and "People's War" in Thailand, 1964–1969* (Berkeley: Center for Chinese Studies, University of California, 1971), p. 78.

[39] Interview with Thanat Khoman, *Bangkok Post*, 5 May 1974.

CHINESE-BUILT ROADS IN LAOS

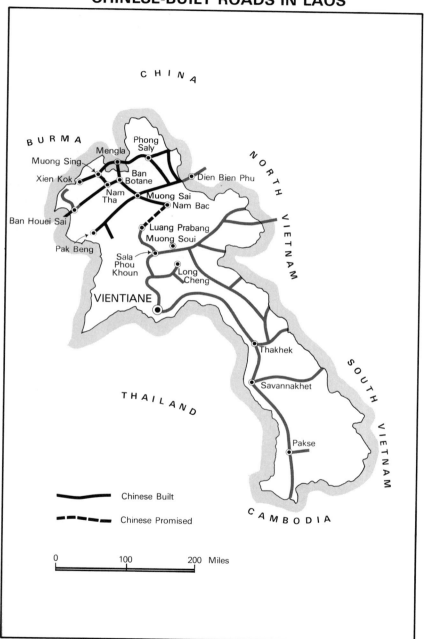

Source: Based on a map in *Far Eastern Economic Review,* 21 February 1975, p. 32.

Thailand in any case: one in the north, dependent upon Peking and supplied via the Chinese-built highway in Laos, and the other in the northeast, heavily dependent on North Vietnam's assistance and located in a region in which large numbers of Vietnamese refugees live.[40]

China's roadbuilding activities in Laos have continued for most of the past decade, and were originally requested by Prince Souvanna Phouma, for purposes of economically linking mountainous northern Laos with the administrative centers of Luang Prabang and, ultimately, Vientiane. The road begins at the Chinese border and has generated concern in Thailand, because by the end of 1974 it was completed to within 100 kilometers of the Thai border. Chinese military construction crews were composed of the same kinds of roadbuilding experts who had repaired North Vietnamese highways north of Hanoi during 1965–1968. They include their own security forces, which have fired upon U.S. reconnaissance aircraft flying over the region in which the Chinese were laboring. The road would give China a capability to move men and supplies into Laos and, presumably, Thailand. And although there has been some speculation that such movement has occurred, the author is aware of no hard evidence which would support such a claim.

Before Peking's reported demurral of further support to the insurgents, both their strength and activities were said to be waxing in all parts of Thailand, although their total number remained under 6,000 active guerrillas. More importantly, they were acquiring more sophisticated firepower and directly attacking regular Thai army units for the first time in the Northeast.[41]

Likewise, the Malayan Communist party has not displayed any diminution in revolutionary fervor with the establishment of diplomatic ties between Kuala Lumpur and Peking. As stated by its clandestine radio transmitter, probably still operating out of China:

Marxism-Leninism holds that the efforts of the socialist countries to strive for peaceful coexistence with countries with differing social systems are one matter, while the revolutionary struggle waged by the peoples of various countries are another. . . . Peaceful coexistence can in no way replace the revolutionary struggle carried out by these peoples. . . . Our present task is to overthrow imperialism

---

[40] Author's interviews in Bangkok, June 1973; and the *Far Eastern Economic Review*, 4 March 1974.

[41] Jeffrey Race, "Thailand 1973: 'We Certainly Have Been Ravaged by Something,'" *Asian Survey*, vol. 14, no. 2 (February 1974), p. 200.

and the reactionary rule of its puppets—the Razak and Lee Kuan Yew cliques—until our nation is completely liberated.

Even after establishing its diplomatic relations with socialist China, the Razak clique will never stop its attacks against the people and the revolutionary forces in our country.[42]

The Malayan Communist party was essentially making two points in the broadcast quoted above. The first, often made by Peking itself, was a separation of state-to-state from interparty relations, thus justifying continued Chinese support for its revolutionary activities. The second was an appeal that support be continued because the MCP was fighting for its survival and that the Malaysian government would not discontinue its pursuit simply because diplomatic relations had been established with the P.R.C. To the contrary, all of the non-Communist Asian governments had made clear their hope that normalized relations with Peking would facilitate their task of wiping out the insurgencies within their territories. And, in recent months, NCNA has rebroadcast statements of the Philippine and Malayan Communist parties, pledging to continue their respective struggles.[43]

The fact that improved state-to-state ties may be less of a guarantee against China's support for local insurgents than regional leaders hope suggests that there may be additional variables affecting Peking's insurgent policy. One of these is clearly the ability of the host government to extend its mandate effectively into the insurgent region. If it cannot, as in the case of Burma, then Chinese leaders may well decide to establish their own lines of control over an important border region *despite* the ostensibly amicable intergovernmental relations. Thus, the pro-Peking Burmese Communist party (BCP) in 1973 employed a 4,000-man army in an attempt to establish a permanent base in the hilly 12,000-square-mile Kengtung area, bordering China, east of the Salween River. Although the BCP had been fighting in this area for some four years, this was the first time that diplomatic, journalistic, and Burmese government reports spoke of Chinese military personnel participating in the campaign, manning both heavy assault weapons and sophisticated communications equipment. BCP troops would retreat to the Chinese sanctuary when the Burmese army sent forces into the region and return after they had gone.[44]

---

[42] Voice of the Malayan Revolution, in Mandarin, 25 May 1974.

[43] NCNA, 9 February and 19 March 1974.

[44] *Far Eastern Economic Review*, 14 January 1974, pp. 22–23; and the *New York Times*, 3 February 1974.

Soviet media have seized upon the disparity between Peking's new friendly state-to-state diplomacy and its continued support for Burmese insurgents and Naga rebels in northeast India as evidence that Peking's blandishments cannot be accepted at face value because its aims remain expansionist.[45]

Nevertheless, there exists a strong incentive for the P.R.C. to encourage overseas Chinese to assimilate and to reduce their insurgent support. China no longer needs their aid on the mainland, and it wishes to set the fears of Asian governments to rest over the fifth column potential of their Chinese residents. Amicable regional ties are essential for Peking in order to undermine Soviet propaganda attempts to rekindle anti-Chinese racism.

Military Capability and Action in Asia

No overview of China's international behavior would be complete without some discussion of the effects of its growing military capability for Asia. Both because of its hostile relationship with Moscow and its understanding that nuclear capability is still the *sine qua non* of great-power status, China has continued to devote considerable resources to military nuclear development (see Table 1). By mid-1973, Western experts estimated that China possessed the following operative missiles: Fifty MRBMs (range 1,500 miles), fifteen-twenty IRBMs (range up to 2,500 miles), and "some" multistage IRBMs (range 3,500 miles). Under development is an ICBM with a range of over 6,000 miles. The MRBMs may be targeted against the Soviet military buildup in Siberia. The IRBMs, including the multistage variety, are probably targeted against European Russia. They could also reach much of Asia, including India.[46]

Peking has also recently increased its transport capability in Tibet, officially for "the economic and political progress of the Tibetan region," by building a 416-meter-long, two-lane bridge across the Brahmaputra River. Only eight miles from India's Northeast Frontier Agency border (the region of China's deepest penetration in 1962), the bridge links a thirty-mile motor road with the Szechwan-Tibet highway. And India fears that, in the event of renewed Sino-Indian hostilities, with the new Kanka bridge Chinese forces could be on Indian soil in a matter of hours.[47] Indeed, China's new

---

[45] Typical is the Moscow *New Times* (4) article of 25 January 1974.

[46] *Far Eastern Economic Review*, 6 May 1974, p. 34.

[47] Brahamanand Mishra, "Fear and Hope Bridge the Brahmaputra," *Far Eastern Economic Review*, 18 March 1974, p. 20.

Table 1

CHINA'S NUCLEAR WEAPON TESTS

Date	Yield	Delivery System	Other Information
10-16-64	20 KT [a]	Ground (tower-mounted)	U-235, implosion device
5-14-65	20–40 KT	Air (TU-4 bomber)	U-235, fission
5-9-66	200–300 KT	Air (TU-16 bomber)	Fission, U-235 and some thermonuclear material (lithium 6)
10-27-66	20–30 KT	Missile (Soviet-type SS4)	Fission, U-235. Missile launched from Shuang Chengtzu over a distance of more than 400 miles
12-28-66	300–500 KT	Ground (tower-mounted	Fission, U-235 and some thermonuclear material (lithium 6)
6-17-67	3 MT [b]	Air (TU-16)	Thermonuclear warhead, fission-fusion-fission type using U-235. Air burst
12-24-67	20–25 KT	Air (TU-16)	Not announced by P.R.C. U-235 and thermonuclear material (lithium 6). Apparently a partial failure with, possibly, only a fission cycle completed
12-27-68	3 MT	Air (TU-16)	Thermonuclear warhead using U-235 and containing some plutonium. Air burst
9-22-69	20–25 KT	——	Fission device, underground test
9-29-69	3 MT	Air (TU-16)	Thermonuclear warhead suitable for ICBM
10-14-70	3 MT	Air (TU-16)	Not announced by P.R.C. Air burst
11-18-71	20 KT	Ground (tower-mounted)	Possibly containing plutonium
1-7-72	Under 20 KT	Air	Possibly containing plutonium. Air burst. Apparently a partial failure
3-18-72	20–200 KT	Air	Possibly a trigger device (containing plutonium) for a thermonuclear warhead. Air burst. Apparently a partial failure
6-27-73	2 MT +	Air	Thermonuclear warhead. Air burst

[a] Kilotons
[b] Megatons
Source: *Far Eastern Economic Review,* 6 May 1974, p. 34.

capability on India's Tibetan border may have motivated a request by an Indian air force delegation in Moscow for the acquisition of long-range Russian strike-fighter aircraft which could penetrate deeply into Tibet.[48]

While an increase in China's nuclear and border transport capabilities has caused some Asian concern for the future, the most dramatic Chinese military action since its 1969 border skirmishing with the Soviet Union occurred not on land or in the air but at sea. The P.R.C. has claimed sovereignty over both the Paracel and Spratley Island groups since 1949, but until January 1974 had never backed its claim with force. At that time a Chinese amphibious force supported by four MiG fighters seized the lightly defended Paracels from South Vietnam. Lying 250 miles east of the South Vietnamese coast and 175 miles south of China's Hainan Island, the Paracels occupy not only a strategic location in the South China Sea between the Straits of Malacca and Japan, where the bulk of Asia's ocean-going commerce moves, but also a location in the middle of an underwater oil, gas, and mineral basin, which is currently being explored and soon may be exploited.[49] Thus, China's occupation of the Paracels and its continued (though contested) claim to the Spratleys, lying further to the southwest, signals its entry into the competitive scramble for undersea resources as well as its strategic concern of protecting its coastal frontier against the growing Soviet naval buildup in the Indian Ocean (to be discussed in Chapter 3).

Peking's advance into the Paracels has resulted in a barely disguised conflict with North Vietnam, which also claims the island group. In a restrained but clearly reproachful statement on the Chinese occupation, "authorized" North Vietnamese sources stated: "The frequently complex disputes over territories and frontiers between neighboring countries demand careful and circumspect examination. . . . Countries involved should settle such disputes by negotiation and in a spirit of equality, mutual respect, friendliness, and good neighborliness."[50]

Some observers have viewed the Chinese attack on the Paracels as a warning to Japan, which has signed an oil development agreement with the R.O.K. in a large area between the southern tip of the Korean peninsula and Japan's southern island of Kyushu. China protested the agreement as an infringement on its sovereignty, since

---

[48] See the report of the talks in *Ananda Bazar Patrika* (Calcutta), 28 April 1974.
[49] Michael Morrow, "Today Hsisha, Tomorrow . . .?" *Far Eastern Economic Review*, 28 January 1974, p. 32.
[50] AFP, 21 January 1974.

it claims the shallow sea above the continental shelf extension. This claim brings China into direct conflict with Taiwan, South Korea, and the Philippines (the latter advancing an archipelago theory that all waters around its islands fall under its jurisdiction). Taiwan has awarded a concession to Japanese petroleum companies for drilling in the Senkaku Islands area between Taiwan and Okinawa. But since the small uninhabited Senkakus are claimed by China and Japan as well, no major drilling has yet begun. Clearly international negotiation is the only answer to these jurisdictional conflicts. And the issues were raised (though not resolved) in the course of the 1974 Law of the Sea Conference.[51]

Moscow seized upon China's military action in the South China Sea to warn of Peking's expansionist aims and chided the Chinese about the delayed disparity between their words and deeds in the South China Sea thrust:

> Peking is particularly fond of talking about the need to defend the rights and interests of small and medium-sized countries and of presenting China as a country which, it is claimed, stands guard over the interests of these countries. But now such countries in Southeast Asia are asking themselves how Peking's verbal assurances can be correlated with her actions and deeds.[52]

The Economic Dimension of Asia's Foreign Policy Environment

Although this is not a study of Asia's international political economy, there is an important economic dimension to its international behavior which affects the larger issue of external power ties to the region. Virtually all non-Communist Asian statesmen agree that the continuation and expansion of international trade and foreign investment are essential for the economic growth and political stability of their respective states. An expanding national product helps satisfy growing consumer demands brought about by the increased urbanization of all Asian states. Foreign investment and markets are necessary for the development of export industries which, in turn, earn the foreign exchange and technology required to sustain the economy's growth and diversification. Because most Asian states have relatively small domestic markets, they are even more dependent on international trade with industrialized partners for development.

---

[51] There is a good discussion of these issues in an article by Fox Butterfield in the *New York Times*, 17 February 1974.

[52] Moscow Domestic Service Roundtable, 27 January 1974.

The usual trade pattern is frequently inimical to small-state control, however, since the latter tends toward high export specialization but diversified import requirements. This exchange renders the small, developing country vulnerable to the economic manipulation of both prices and product quantity by the larger states.[53] Since World War II, it has meant that, with the exception of fossil fuels and certain scarce minerals such as tungsten and uranium, the earnings of primary product exporters have steadily diminished when compared with the prices they must pay for high technology imports.

While the skyrocketing world demand for oil has benefited such petroleum exporters as Iran, Indonesia, and to a smaller extent, Malaysia, and world grain shortages may benefit a rice exporter like Thailand, generally the Asian states, as much of the third world, suffer from the energy-demand explosion. Because they are least able to pay the inflated energy prices prevailing since 1973, countries such as India have not only had to postpone economic development plans but have also incurred cutbacks in basic necessities, including grain and fertilizer production.[54] Those few countries which are reaping windfall profits from their petroleum exports will face growing demands from their regional partners for some share of the wealth and for preferential access or prices.

In at least one case, that of Iran, large oil profits have been translated into military wherewithal and growing political influence. The shah spent more than $3 billion on weapons in 1973 alone, to insure Iran's domination of the Persian Gulf and the ability of its navy to patrol as far south as Madagascar. Iran's navy possesses the largest hovercraft fleet in the world, with the capability to move a battalion almost anywhere in the gulf in a matter of hours. Its air force is being equipped with laser-guided bombs and KC-135 aerial tankers to refuel more than 100 F-4 Phantoms. Its 16,000-man ground force now has 700 new U.S. support helicopters; 800 new British Chieftain tanks with the world's most advanced fire-control system are to be added to an extant force of 1,000 American tanks and an air wing of C-130 transports. Observers predict that the shah will have purchased over $9 billion worth of weapons from the United

---

[53] Vital, *Inequality of States*, p. 54.

[54] For a good general discussion of the differing capabilities of the developed and developing countries to adjust to inflated energy prices, see William E. Griffith, "The Fourth Middle East War, The Energy Crisis, and U.S. Policy," *Orbis*, vol. 17, no. 4 (Winter 1974).

States by 1980.[55] This kind of military development cannot help but affect the security planning of both India and the Soviet Union, which perceive Iran as sympathetic to Pakistan and the United States. In short, the shah's military buildup in the Persian Gulf, made possible by the oil earnings he is striving militarily to protect, may well be the impetus for a competitive arms race in both the gulf region and the western Indian Ocean. (More will be said on this subject in Chapter 3.)

---

[55] NBC-TV Special Report on the Persian Gulf, 24 February 1974; and David Holden, "Shah of Shahs, Shah of Dreams," *New York Times Magazine*, 26 May 1974, p. 42.

2
FACTORS INHIBITING
ASIAN COOPERATION

The neutralization of a world region requires consensus on the part of its members and the major external powers over the sources of instability within the region, the nature of external threat, and the optimal policy for dealing with both. There are a number of features in the Asian scene inhibiting the development of such a consensus, however. The most important include ethnic distrust within and between states, dissension over the distribution of power within the region as the Indochina conflict terminates, and the question of freedom of the seas versus territorial waters for archipelago Southeast Asia—this last issue containing broader implications for both external access and economic development through international commerce. This chapter will consider each of these factors in turn.

Ethnic Disputes

Perhaps no other region in the world contains the human diversity of Southeast Asia, for centuries a crossroads of religions and tribal peoples moving in all directions. The modern outcome of this history of mobility is a mixture of differences, which, for the most part, has not led to a synthesis but remains at worst something of a boiling cauldron of incompatible elements, seething against each other and, at best, a mosaic of different components which uneasily cohabit the same framework. The languages spoken in Southeast Asia are more numerous than the region's countries; religions express radically different world views, from the quietism of Buddhism and Taoism to the evangelistic fervor and worldly orientations of Islam and Christianity. Strains within the region encompass both religious and ethnic issues, for example: (1) the dispute between Malaysia and Thailand over the conversion to Buddhism of ethnic Malays in southern Thailand, which is inhibiting bilateral cooperation over the suppression of insurgents in the border region, (2) the violence between Muslim insurgents and potential secessionists in the southern Philippines and the Catholic majority, and (3) concern over the forced Islamization of Sabah tribesmen.[1]

The ethnic components of interstate conflict in mainland Southeast Asia grew out of the European colonial practice of viewing rivers as convenient boundaries rather than as transportation arteries. Thus, the Mekong, for example, divides Thailand and Laos even though such a division leaves more Lao in Thailand than in Laos itself and creates the basis for Thai concern over the loyalty of its border region inhabitants. A plausible scenario for endemic regional conflict is inherent in this situation, with central governments employing force to control minorities near their borders and the latter responding by appealing for assistance from fellow ethnics in neighboring countries.[2] Ethnic suspicions are exacerbated, of course, when neighboring countries are composed not only of differing people but also of what is perceived to be a hostile and aggressive political system, as, for example, Thailand views North Vietnam and the Communist-controlled areas of Laos. This kind of instability cannot be contained militarily. Rather, the problem is one of creating a new sense of national loyalty in the prospect of social improvement for resident minorities. Without such prospects, they are, indeed, a latent fifth column.

Looking more closely at the situation in Thailand, in many ways the most complex of the region, one discovers insurgency problems on all four of the country's international borders: Cambodia, Laos, Burma, and Malaysia. In each case the problem's persistence grows out of an inability of the central government of each state to extend its mandate into these regions, although the specific nature of the insurgency varies. The potentially most troublesome to Thailand are the Communist-supported struggles in its North and Northeast supplied through Laos and possibly Cambodia, now that the Khmer Rouge has overthrown the Lon Nol government.

The least important of Thailand's border difficulties is with Burma, primarily because the insurgents on that border are uninter-

---

[1] For a good discussion of these divisions, see Margaret Roff, "Disintegration and Integration in Southeast Asia," *Columbia Essays in International Affairs: The Dean's Papers, 1971*, vol. 7 (New York: Columbia University Press, 1972).

[2] Jerry M. Silverman, "Historic National Rivalries and Interstate Conflict in Mainland Southeast Asia," in Milne and Zacher, eds., *Conflict and Stability*, pp. 45–78.

ested in fomenting unrest in Thailand. They are Lahu and Shan rebels against Rangoon, who have used Thailand for sanctuary from the periodic forays against them by the Burmese army. Both Rangoon and Bangkok have acted (through joint consultation in August 1973) to keep these border difficulties under control.[3]

Moving up the scale of Thai concern, one comes to the southern border with Malaysia. Bangkok's Communist Suppression Operation Command (CSOC) estimated some 2,000 insurgents in the far south, still oriented toward Malaysia and led by the legendary Chin Peng, who headed the Communist revolt in Malaya in the 1950s. The insurgents may have irredentist ambitions for Thailand's four southern provinces, although the Malaysian government denies any such interest.[4] More recently, however, reports have circulated of a southern insurgent willingness to negotiate with the Thai government over the status of Muslims in Thailand. The basic issues appear to be a better system of justice, more tax allocation for development, and decentralized local administration.[5]

The most important of the insurgencies are located on the Laotian border in the North and Northeast. Intelligence sources in Bangkok estimate a maximum of 7,500 Communist Terrorists in the two regions, dominated by the Meo and other tribesmen in the North, although led by native Thai and Sino-Thai cadres. Observers claim that the northern insurgencies are waxing with the support of several thousand villagers who, as in South Vietnam, provide intelligence to the rebels, which enables them to elude Thai military operations.[6] Many of the villagers in the Northeast are Vietnamese, adding an ethnic dimension to the rebellion. Northeastern provincial officials are convinced that the 40,000 resident Vietnamese in their provinces provide the financial and intelligence backbone for the insurgency, although they admit an absence of hard evidence.[7] Further, a 1974 U.S. intelligence study argued that North Vietnam has emplaced a complex logistical system to support rural revolt in Thailand. According to the study, the system is manned by 2,000 North Vietnamese and Pathet Lao troops and stretches from North Vietnam through

[3] John A. Wiant, "Burma 1973: New Turns in the Burmese Way to Socialism," *Asian Survey*, vol. 14, no. 2 (February 1974), pp. 175–176.

[4] Robert Shaplen, "Letter from Thailand," *The New Yorker*, 14 January 1974, p. 82. The CSOC was renamed Internal Security Operations Command in late 1974.

[5] *The Nation* (Bangkok), 8 February 1974.

[6] Ibid.

[7] David Jenkins, "Thailand's Enduring Dilemma," *Far Eastern Economic Review*, 30 April 1973, p. 27.

the Communist-controlled areas of Laos and Cambodia and into the Thai provinces adjoining the latter two countries.[8]

American analysts disagree over whether the two northern insurgencies are separate—the northern Maoist and the Vietminh-backed northeastern guerrillas.[9] According to some, the northern insurgency is a Maoist phenomenon, emphasizing collective farming and refusing to form a united front with other locals in opposition to Bangkok. Its support and training are alleged to emanate from Chinese road-building activities in Laos. One explanation for a separate Chinese-supported Thai insurgency is a kind of insurance of influence in Thailand vis-à-vis the Vietminh once all of Indochina ultimately comes under D.R.V. domination.

The alternate viewpoint treats both insurgencies as essentially identical, arguing that the cadres, training, and support are the same, and that adherents of both claim membership in the Thai Communist party. Most analysts agree, however, that the insurgents are acting on their own rather than as agents for either Hanoi or Peking and that they look to the former as mentors rather than leaders.

The Thai Communists have exploited local economic grievances through a socio-political program which encourages northern villagers to take local government into their own hands. This emphasis on local initiative is then compared with the venality of many central government province representatives and the unwillingness of Bangkok to allocate significant developmental resources to the region. Insofar as the Communists are able to organize the villagers to deal with their own problems, these natives are provided with a political role and a sense of participation for the first time in their lives. This is particularly appealing to the young, who have been prime targets of the insurgent campaign. For them, joining the insurgents provides upward mobility, a sense of status, and immediate benefits.

Until the Sanya government began to reorganize the CSOC in 1974, the Thai military refused to develop a separate paramilitary elite unit to operate in the North and Northeast. The reason for its lack of response may be found in the Thai tradition of coup politics and the concern of the military leadership over the creation of any new force which could be employed to bring down an incumbent government. Thus, the exigencies of Thai armed forces politics—deployment to

---

[8] The study is cited by Jeffrey Race, "Thailand in 1974: A New Constitution," *Asian Survey*, vol. 15, no. 2 (February 1975), p. 164.

[9] The following discussion is drawn from the author's interviews in Bangkok, June 1973.

protect current powerholders—proved unfunctional to the control of internal insurgencies far from the capital.

Although the Sanya government did not develop a definitive policy toward the insurgents, it at least jettisoned the old. Puai Ungphakon, economic advisor to former Prime Minister Sanya, urged the government to negotiate with the rebels to learn if some accommodation could be reached. And the prime minister himself, in June 1974, established land committees with the authority to investigate tenant grievances against landlords and impose summary settlements through land reallocation or cash payments.[10] (More will be presented on this subject below, in the analysis of the outcome of the Indochina conflict.)

The last major ethnic dispute in Southeast Asia meriting consideration is the Muslim rebellion in southern Mindanao and the Sulu islands. In a sense, this issue surpasses the Thai insurgencies in its implications for regional cooperation because it involves the issue of Malaysian clandestine support for Philippine rebels and hence challenges the basic viability of ASEAN.

The Philippines' 2.5 million Muslims are predominantly found in the southern islands, 500 miles from Manila. Estimates of the insurgents run as high as 12,000, loosely organized in separate bands.[11] The character of the rebellion varies with the different regions involved. In some areas, such as Cotabato Province on Mindanao, the dispute takes on a distinctly Christian versus Muslim cast because of the struggle over land between the original Muslim farmers and the increasing number of Christian settlers moving from more densely populated islands to the north. But in other areas, such as the Sulu island chain, it has little to do with religious differences, since there are few resident Christians. Overlaying religious differences about land ownership is a complex of grievances against the relationship worked out between Manila and local politicians, who have continued to rule in the old manner of the original sultans, using private armies and backdoor deals to expand their personal fiefdoms at the expense of the local populace.

The Marcos government has used both carrot and stick tactics to break the rebellion, with only indifferent success. Along with military assaults on rebel sanctuaries have come amnesty offers and recon-

---

[10] The *Bangkok Post*, 21 April and 5 June 1974.

[11] This discussion draws heavily from the following accounts: Sydney H. Schanberg, "Philippine Moslem Army: Separate Bands with Single Aim of Independence," *New York Times*, 1 April 1974; and the *Far Eastern Economic Review*, 25 March 1974, pp. 12–14.

struction loans and grants. In a May 1974 summit meeting with Indonesian President Suharto, Marcos promised that the southern Filipinos would regain the land of their forefathers—though the method and timing of such a land transfer was not elaborated.[12]

The regional aspect of unrest in the southern Philippines concerns allegations which have been made by Filipinos just below the official level that the Malaysian state of Sabah has been providing crucial military support for the rebels. Captured insurgents, according to Philippine sources, admit being trained in Sabah by regular members of the Malaysian armed forces and then conveyed in Malaysian military vehicles to drop-off points in the Sulu Islands.[13]

The people of Sulu and eastern Sabah are tied by blood and cultural origins. After the sanguinary siege of Jolo city in Mindanao in January 1974, the number of Philippine Muslim refugees in Sabah climbed to almost 25,000. The Malaysian government extended refuge on humanitarian grounds but vigorously denied providing any assistance to the secessionist movement.[14] There has been some speculation that Malaysian support for the Philippine insurgents may be a pressure tactic designed to elicit an agreement from Manila to drop its longstanding claim to sovereignty over Sabah in exchange for a cessation of Malaysian support of the rebels. When asked about this possibility, the Philippine president neither confirmed nor denied it.[15]

Despite the potential for bitter public recriminations in the Sabah–southern Philippine dispute, relations between the two governments have remained remarkably cordial at the public level. President Marcos has invited representatives of the International Islamic Secretariat located in Kuala Lumpur to visit the Philippines and observe conditions in the south firsthand. He has also entertained visits by Arab officials. The Malaysian government has declared that the difficulties are an internal matter of the Philippines. And both Indonesia and Malaysia have backed Manila's position in international conferences in order to maintain ASEAN solidarity.[16]

Nevertheless, Singapore Prime Minister Lee Kwan Yew has noted with alarm that assistance to insurgents of one country by another,

---

[12] *Antara* (Jakarta), 30 May 1974.

[13] Author's interviews in Manila, May 1973; and the *Far Eastern Economic Review*, 25 March 1974, pp. 12–14.

[14] AFP (Hong Kong), 12 March 1974.

[15] AFP (Hong Kong), 31 May 1974.

[16] Author interview with Professor Estrella Solidum, University of the Philippines and member of the Philippines ASEAN delegation, Manila, May 1973.

whatever the motivation, is a very dangerous game, for it undercuts the very essence of regional self-reliance and mutual trust necessary for an indigenous security arrangement in a depolarizing Asia. He said further that "if forces extraneous to the region are allowed through connivance or abetment to advance their influence for ideological, religious, or irredentist reasons, through the supply of money and arms, then the great powers will soon get into the act, and get into it much more effectively." [17] Given the persistence of the regional disputes discussed above, in addition to those only mentioned in passing (such as the Communist insurgency on the Sabah-Sarawak border with Indonesia and the ever-present Indo-Pakistani distrust, inhibiting the formation of a South Asian security community), this question clearly remains unanswered: can endemic differences be transcended in the larger interest of regional integrity?

Non-Communist Asia's View of the Indochina Conflict Outcome

There was no opportunity to develop and test exclusively indigenous regional security arrangements in Asia before some disposition of the Indochina conflict had occurred. The residual U.S. military presence (exclusively air and naval) on mainland Southeast Asia was premised on the continuation of the war. It was designed as an inducement to Hanoi to comply with the January 1973 Paris Agreement insofar as the progressive withdrawal of U.S. forces was based on a diminution of military hostilities and a movement toward a negotiated settlement between North and South Vietnam. For the remainder of non-Communist Asia, the ultimate political disposition of Indochina comprises its proximate regional security setting and requirements. The implication of a Vietminh-dominated Indochina versus a Balkanization solution may be quite different for the security planners of ASEAN and other states. The purpose of this section is to examine the varying ways in which Asian analysts themselves relate the outcome of the Indochina war to their security requirements. Because the salience of the war varies directly with geographical distance, the country to which most attention is given will be Thailand. As the only exclusively mainland member of ASEAN with borders abutting on Indochina, Thailand is potentially a security link between mainland and archipelago Southeast Asia.

Mainland Southeast Asia's overriding concern with defense has been documented by Stephen Chee, who pointed out that between

---

[17] AFP, 31 May 1974.

34 and 50 percent of its national budgets were spent on defense, while the corresponding figure for the archipelago was 15 to 30 percent. The persistence of war as a social process in the region holds additional implications. It has led to the development of the military as the strongest organization in most of the region and, until the Thai student revolution of October 1973, seven of the ten Southeast Asian states had military-dominated governments.[18] Indeed, the maintenance of strong military establishments, ostensibly against external threat (or domestic dissidence), is becoming increasingly perceived by Southeast Asia's educated youth as a way of suppressing legitimate societal grievances and remaining in power.[19] This viewpoint is reinforced by analysts who argue that the external Communist element within regional insurgencies has been overemphasized and that most of the insurgencies are less the products of machinations from Hanoi and Peking than they are ethnic, tribal, religious, and in some cases, separatist grievances. Furthermore, insofar as the insurgents can be identified as beholden to outside Communist forces, local nationalist sentiments can be mobilized against them.[20]

The effect of the Indochina war's outcome on regional security is complicated by the fact that, until the American withdrawal from direct participation in 1973, the war was not so much a regional phenomenon as a global one in a regional setting. States outside Southeast Asia (China, the United States, and the U.S.S.R.) played major and, in some cases, determinative roles. Even with American disengagement the Indochina conflict has not been assessed as a *regional* problem but rather as a series of separate national concerns. In part, this lack of regional planning reflects the paucity of institutions in Southeast Asia which provide a common viewpoint. And, in fairness, it should be noted that the one regional political institution currently operating in Asia—ASEAN—has recognized the disposition of Indochina as a critical issue for its members. At its sixth foreign-ministers meeting in Bangkok in April 1973, ASEAN proposed reconstruction assistance to Indochina. The ASEAN states, however, have no real influence on either the Indochina actors or their outside supporters. And a Communist-controlled Indochina would directly threaten only one ASEAN member—Thailand. Nevertheless, the potential for mischief throughout the region would be considerable

---

[18] Stephen H. C. Chee, "Problems and Prospects in Southeast Asia," in *Issues for the Seventies* (Kuala Lumpur: NESEC Seminar for Student Leaders, 1973), p. 21.
[19] Author's seminar discussion at the Institute of Southeast Asian Studies, Singapore, 5 June 1973.
[20] Clough, "East Asia," p. 53; and J. L. S. Girling, "A Neutral Southeast Asia?" *Australian Outlook*, vol. 27, no. 2 (August 1973), p. 128.

when Hanoi unifies Vietnam under its control. As Lee Kwan Yew put it, the weapons captured by the Vietminh in a South Vietnam victory could supply regional insurgents for years, with virtually no need for additional support from either Peking or Moscow.[21]

My own observations in the spring and summer of 1973 suggested that many Southeast Asians desired the continuation of a U.S. military presence on mainland Southeast Asia at least until the Indochina hostilities terminated, but that they were skeptical about whether the Americans would, in fact, elect to stay. It was the lack of assurance over a sustained U.S. commitment that led to the ASEAN neutralization proposal and to separate national military buildup decisions, such as Malaysia's 1973 purchase of two F-5 fighter squadrons.[22]

The gradual winding down of the U.S. commitment to Indochina presented Thailand with some fundamental policy questions: Of what utility are U.S. bases against local insurgents? Of what utility are U.S. bases against a hostile North Vietnam? Even if the Thai government decided to request the retention of U.S. forces in the country, what is the probability that the United States would comply?

Addressing the last question first, the ambiguities of the Nixon Doctrine concerning the permanent posting of U.S. military personnel on mainland Asia, plus the general antipathy of the U.S. Congress toward American overseas involvement, reduced the likelihood in the minds of many observers that the United States can maintain a long-term military presence in Thailand. In September 1969, the Senate unanimously passed a resolution which, in effect, superseded the 1962 Rusk-Thanat understanding on U.S. security guarantees to Thailand outside the SEATO contract. The Senate resolution insisted that no American ground forces be employed in the event of war in Thailand. Although the Nixon administration disavowed the Senate statement, most Thais viewed it as the beginning of the end of a reliable American security guarantee.[23] Nevertheless, in 1974, some 30,000 U.S. Air Force personnel remained in the country, as well as elements of the Seventh Fleet at Sattahip.

What purposes do the U.S. bases serve for the Thais? Both Thai and American officials state publicly that the bases are not for use against insurgent movements operating in Thailand. Yet the

---

[21] See the insightful article by George C. Thomson, "Southeast Asia after the Ceasefire," *Asian Affairs*, November-December 1973.

[22] Author's discussions with Asian and American officials and academics in the five ASEAN capitals, May-June 1973.

[23] Bernard Brodie, *Strategy and National Interests* (New York: National Strategy Information Center, 1971), p. 22.

presence of 2,000 guerrillas near the U.S. airbase at Nokhan Phonom suggests the insurgents think otherwise.[24] Professional observers claim that the Thai leadership has viewed the bases as constituting a kind of transitional insurance policy to deter the North Vietnamese from any plans they may have to step up their aid to the northern insurgencies.[25] Both Thai and American officials seem to agree that the bases are "temporary" and that the number of U.S. troops depends on the situation in the region—that is, how well the Americans believed the North Vietnamese were living up to the Paris accord by reducing the military level of the Indochina conflict.

The October 1973 change of government in Bangkok brought with it no apparent change in the rationale for the American military presence.[26] And even the Thai press, which had become increasingly critical through 1974 about U.S. operations in Thailand, has defended Bangkok's continued membership in SEATO, on the grounds that it is the only treaty organization that will protect the country against an act of open aggression.[27]

There is, however, a kind of "chicken-egg" relationship between the U.S. bases in Thailand and Bangkok's association with Hanoi. That is, Thailand and North Vietnam each predicate improved contacts between themselves with a change in behavior by the other, but neither seemed willing to initiate the process before Indochina fell to the Communists. The Vietnamese Communist bill of particulars against Thailand included not only the standard allegations that the U.S. Air Force was engaged in combat over Indochina from Thai bases in violation of the Paris Agreement, but also that "the United States has created on Thai territory centers to train military and police forces for its henchmen, formed an apparatus to train and command special forces to carry out activities throughout Southeast Asia and established a center to direct an intelligence network to carry out long-range sabotage activities in neighboring countries." In other words, Hanoi was making the case that the U.S. intends to remain involved in Indochina, to resist North Vietnamese hegemony, and to use Thailand as the base for its operations. In conclusion, Hanoi asserts that there can be no improvement in D.R.V.-Thai relations until all U.S. bases and forces are withdrawn.[28]

---

[24] Thomson, "Southeast Asia after the Ceasefire," p. 102.

[25] Author's interviews in Bangkok, June 1973.

[26] See, for example, the interview with Defense Minister Thawi Chunlasap in *The Nation* (Bangkok), 14 January 1974.

[27] *Bangkok Post* editorial, 4 March 1974.

[28] Typical is the commentary found in North Vietnam's military newspaper, *Quan Doi Nhan Dan*, which was broadcast by Hanoi Radio on 31 May 1974.

Thai officials expressed a willingness to negotiate with Hanoi on the total withdrawal of U.S. forces as well as on the treatment of some 70,000 Vietnamese refugees resident in the country. But prior to the January 1975 national elections, the Thais insisted that the withdrawal of American troops would occur only after North Vietnam had withdrawn its forces from Laos and Cambodia.[29] Both Thais and Americans made token gestures of good faith to Hanoi, the latter reducing the number of B-52s stationed in Thailand and the former offering for the first time to provide Thai citizenship to those Vietnamese who desire it and possess a record of "good behavior."[30] Thanat Khoman, ex-foreign minister and current advisor to the former prime minister, is one of the foremost advocates of improving relations with Hanoi as the best way of insuring the cessation of North Vietnamese aid to the Thai insurgents. Adopting the logic of the Malaysian government in its decision to establish diplomatic relations with China, Thanat argues "that if you reach understanding with the sources of support for insurgency or for Communist illegal activities, then the illegal activities stop."[31]

Moreover, the Thai press became very sensitive to what it perceives as a lack of U.S. consultation on the use of its bases within the country. The press has castigated unilateral U.S. Defense Department statements about the length of time the bases will be in operation and against whom they might be used. One reporter complained: "It is obvious that Thailand's policy on this issue is dependent on U.S. interests rather than on those of the Thai people. This is the main reason why North Vietnam still maintains such a hostile attitude toward Thailand."[32] And when a U.S. Marine contingent was sent to Thailand in May 1975 to participate in the recapture of the U.S. merchant ship *Mayaguez* from the Cambodian Communists, the Thai government sternly protested both the presence of the Marines and the lack of American consultation.

The January 1975 elections led to the formation of a government in March under Premier Kukrit Pramoj. In a seven-party coalition arrangement, which required the support of some leftists to win the necessary majority, the new prime minister articulated a policy which would require the withdrawal of U.S. forces from Thailand by

---

[29] The *Bangkok Post*, 30 May 1974 and an interview with Deputy Foreign Minister Chatchai in *The Nation*, 4 June 1974.

[30] The *Bangkok Post*, 7 June 1974.

[31] Interview with Thanat Khoman in the *Bangkok Post*, 5 May 1974.

[32] Kafae Dam article in *Siam Rat*, 16 April 1974.

March 1976.[33] The fall of Cambodia and South Vietnam to the Communists in April 1975 accelerated the Thai policy of dissociation from the United States. Thai leaders clearly believe that any further U.S. military presence is provocative to the Vietnamese. As an earnest of Bangkok's good intentions toward its potentially hostile neighbors, Prime Minister Kukrit is negotiating the complete removal of U.S. military personnel from his country, although the future status of American access to the important Satahip naval complex has not been mentioned. Diplomatically, Thailand appears to be moving closer to Peking in hopes of balancing Hanoi's all too apparent distrust and hostility.

The whole insurgency issue is complicated by past Thai military involvement in Laos and Bangkok concern that a neighbor dominated by the Pathet Lao would find the prospect of aiding insurgents so close to its borders irresistible. Up to thirty battalions of "Thai volunteers" had fought on the Vietnam side in the Laotian segment of the Indochina war with U.S. financing. With the initialing of a Laotian ceasefire and subsequent coalition government agreement, Bangkok claimed that all Thai forces were withdrawn from Laos by the spring of 1974.

But Thai officials complained that North Vietnamese and Pathet Lao forces had set up bases in the area of Laos adjacent to the Mekong River border of Thailand opposite the Tha U-then district and just twenty kilometers from Nakhon Phanom. The Thai district governor estimated the presence of some 10,000 Communist troops across the river in Laos.[34] The Pathet Lao radio denied any interference in Thailand and countercharged that the Thai administration was reorganizing its troops in Laos and mixing them with Vientiane forces. This allegation was echoed by Thai insurgent propagandists.[35]

The question arises: can any other arrangement take the place of a U.S. security guarantee after the Indochina war? Some Thai believe that ASEAN might be able to play such a role over time.[36] Bangkok had been in the vanguard of those who wished to see ASEAN play a larger part in helping to bring about a negotiated settlement. (Indonesia is the other ASEAN activist on this issue, though for reasons of national prestige rather than security.) In the 1974 annual

---

[33] "Thais to Ask U.S. for Speedier Exit," *New York Times*, 4 March 1975, and "Thai's New Cabinet Wins Its First Test in Parliament," ibid., 20 March 1975.

[34] Bangkok Domestic Service in Thai, 2 March 1974.

[35] Radio Pathet Lao, 22 April 1974; and the Voice of the People of Thailand, 4 June 1974.

[36] Author's discussion with foreign policy specialist, Professor Sumsoth, of Chulalongkorn University, 20 June 1973.

foreign ministers meeting, as in 1973, Thai Foreign Minister Charunphan urged the convocation of a ten-nation Southeast Asian conference to include in addition to ASEAN, Burma, Laos, Cambodia, and the two Vietnams.[37] Persistent Thai appeals for a larger gathering to include mainland states reflected the fact that it is the only member of ASEAN *directly* threatened by a Communist victory in Indochina. Thus, Thailand has consistently encouraged greater ASEAN concern over mainland developments. According to one American observer, however, Thai efforts in this direction have not been particularly successful because of the general belief among the region's foreign-policy elites that Indochina will become a North Vietnamese sphere of influence. The reaction to this belief is that some organization of Asian non-Communist states (perhaps ASEAN) will have to deal through Hanoi insofar as it wants to relate to a postwar Indochina.[38]

If the above is an accurate exploration of Asian views of the outcome of the Indochina war, then Thailand may be less concerned about China's road building, the reported presence of 24,000 Chinese troops in northern Laos, and even China's relations with Thailand's own northern insurgents. A Chinese presence in the region could deny the Vietminh exclusive access to the insurgencies, thus providing Peking with some influence on North Vietnamese behavior. This line of analysis suggests that China is interested less in harassing Bangkok than in maintaining a modicum of influence in a strategic border region so that the D.R.V. may not become the sole external backer.[39] And, indeed, the Thai National Assembly's December 1974 decision to repeal its trade embargo against China may be seen in the broader context of improving political relations with a power possessing some influence in Hanoi. It should be pointed out, however, that much of the preceding discussion on Thailand's regional policy options is quite speculative in that none of the major contenders for leadership in the January 1975 national elections has really articulated a full-blown foreign policy position; and the Sanya caretaker government operated very cautiously in order not to commit its popularly elected successor.

The 1974 Laotian agreement on coalition government and Balkanization of the country may be more satisfactory to Thailand

---

[37] *Bangkok Post*, 8 May 1974.

[38] Remarks by Professor Donald Weatherbee, based on interviews in Southeast Asia in the summer of 1973, at the Seminar Workshop on North Vietnam and the Security of Southeast Asia, University of South Carolina Institute of International Studies, October 1973.

[39] Author's interviews in Bangkok, June 1973.

and China, then, than it is to North Vietnam. A Balkanized Laos, with the Pathet Lao in control of most of the east and the non-Communists occupying most of the Mekong River side of Laos, would permit the country to serve as a reasonably satisfactory buffer between Thailand and North Vietnam. Should the coalition arrangement serve merely as a way station toward total Pathet Lao control, however, then Thailand's border problems may be only beginning, and China's incentive to step up its influence will be increased.[40]

The Straits/National Waters Concept vs. Freedom of the Seas

Before concluding this chapter on factors inhibiting regional cooperation, we must examine a legal, commercial, and strategic dispute that divides both the ASEAN states and the great powers. This dispute is part of a larger global controversy discussed at the 1974 Law of the Sea Conference, and concerns questions of what constitute territorial waters for both passage and exploitation purposes and what are the laws regulating the usage of international straits, especially by warships. For our purposes, the legal aspects of the controversy are largely ignored; the focus instead is on its political implications for regional cooperation, because national positions on the use of Southeast Asia's waters are wrapped up in questions of regional status and control.

Part of the controversy over the use of Asian waters is illustrative of a growing ambiguity in great power/small power relations. In the past many smaller states were prized by larger powers with global fleets for their base location. The importance of these locations has diminished with decolonization and growing nationalist resentment over foreign enclaves in third world countries. More recently, many littoral states have begun to claim wide maritime zones (in some cases up to 200 miles) adjoining their coasts which the great naval powers perceive as both economic and strategic obstacles to their use of the world's oceans and seas. Small power attempts to control the narrow passageways between great bodies of salt water (to be discussed below) are especially repugnant to major naval states, particularly if, as in the case of Japan, they are dependent upon the unimpeded use of these straits for economic survival. Japan's de-

---

[40] See the insightful chapter by Kenneth P. Landon, "The Impact of the Sino-American Detente on the Indochina Conflict," in Gene T. Hsiao, ed., *Sino-American Detente* (New York: Praeger Special Studies Series in International Politics, 1974), pp. 218–220. By May 1975 it appeared that the Pathet Lao were on their way to assuming complete control of the country.

pendence on free straits passage is exacerbated by the fact that it possesses neither the capability nor intention of escorting its merchant ships beyond its own territorial waters and is consequently completely dependent upon the good will of littoral states.[41]

Perhaps the key issue of dispute concerns usage of the Straits of Malacca between the east coast of Sumatra and the west coast of the Malay peninsula. Along with the adjoining Straits of Singapore, they comprise part of the shortest sea route between the Indian Ocean and the South China Sea. The width of the straits varies from 3.2 nautical miles (nm) in the Straits of Singapore to 11.1 nm at the eastern outlet. Over 40,000 vessels per year pass through the straits, including more than 8,000 tankers bound mostly for Japan. In 1971, seventy of these tankers were over 200,000 dead weight tons (DWT).[42]

It was in part a concern over marine pollution by the ubiquitous tanker traffic which led Malaysia and Indonesia to claim jointly in November 1971 that the straits would be considered their national waters rather than an international waterway. Some analysts attributed the initiative for the declarations to Indonesia, growing out of its archipelago concept of national waters first proclaimed in 1960.[43] As an island nation, Indonesia (and recently the Philippines) has claimed that the seas connecting its land members are territorial waters. Since the Straits of Malacca provide direct access to Indonesia, Jakarta, along with Kuala Lumpur, declared a twelve-mile boundary, thus asserting joint control over marine traffic in what the two capitals view as territorial waters. The joint claim may have been precipitated by a July 1971 Japanese Ministry of Transport proposal to the United Nations that navigation through the straits be made the responsibility of the UN's Intergovernmental Marine Consultative Group.[44]

Singapore was caught in the middle of the Indonesian-Malaysian initiative. Its politico-strategic requirement of maintaining good relations with its two large Malay neighbors was in direct conflict with its economic status as the major entrepôt in Southeast Asia whose bunkering and shipping facilities depended on unimpeded access.

---

[41] See the discussion by Frank C. Langdon, "Japanese Policy toward Southeast Asia," in Milne and Zacher, Conflict and Stability, p. 341.

[42] Cited in M. Pathmanatham, "The Straits of Malacca: A Basis for Conflict or Cooperation?" in Lau Teak Soon, ed., New Directions in the International Relations of Southeast Asia (Singapore University Press, 1973), p. 186.

[43] Michael Leifer and Dolliver Nelson, "Conflict of Interest in the Straits of Malacca," International Affairs (London), vol. 49, no. 2 (April 1973), p. 191.

[44] Ibid., p. 192.

On 3 March 1972, a week after Nixon left China, the Soviet Union, through its Tokyo ambassador, and the Japanese foreign minister both declared that the Straits of Malacca must be considered international waters. (Both the American and Soviet navies had transited the straits during the Bangladesh War in December 1971.) Kuala Lumpur and Jakarta responded immediately by reiterating their earlier position and going on to claim the right to search any vessel passing through the straits and to object to any ships carrying arms to unfriendly countries. To fill out the diplomatic standoff, soon thereafter the chairman of the U.S. Joint Chiefs of Staff, Admiral Thomas Moorer, issued a statement comparable to the declaration of Japan and the U.S.S.R. In a sense the United States was even more specific by objecting to what Indonesia and Malaysia termed the "right of innocent passage" because the littoral states could treat it at their own discretion, and, in any case, it would cover neither aircraft nor submerged submarines.[45]

In an attempt to assuage possible pollution objections resulting from maritime accident, Japan offered to dredge the straits and fit the main channel with radar buoys. Jakarta and Kuala Lumpur rejected the offer, urging instead that ships over 200,000 DWT use alternative routes through the Makassar and Lombok straits, a journey which would add three to four days to Yokohama. In any case, tankers above 300,000 DWT cannot use the Malacca Straits. In order to make the Makassar-Lombok route more attractive, Indonesia has offered the use of Lombok Island and Tiluk Semongka to foreign oil producers as depot sites. Harbors there could accommodate ships of up to 550,000 DWT.[46] In 1973 Japan and Indonesia undertook a joint survey of the Lombok-Makassar route, agreeing on its feasibility despite increased time and costs.

Singaporean officials point out that the Indonesian-Malaysian assertion of control over the Straits of Malacca is a hollow one, since neither state has the capability of closing the passageway to outside powers. Moreover, should the littoral states split over whether an outside navy may pass, a conflict is bound to occur which would threaten regional harmony and encourage the exercise of external influence on the disputants. In short, an unenforceable claim to control who transits the straits can lead only to unnecessary regional disputation. By contrast, a general position of free passage for all would minimize the possibility of disputes between the littoral states

[45] Ibid., p. 198.

[46] *Asian Student* (San Francisco), 17 October 1973. See also the *Straits Times* (Kuala Lumpur), 25 May 1973.

and external powers.[47] That this is a sensible position was underlined when both Soviet and American naval vessels transited the straits in November 1973 and refused to honor the Indonesian/Malaysian "innocent passage" policy by requesting permission. The Indonesian government "deplored and regretted" the incidents but did nothing.[48] In recognition of this naval weakness, Indonesian Navy chief of staff, Admiral Subaro, announced that Jakarta would undertake to create an international waters capability for the first time and that by 1979 Indonesia would possess a destroyer and two other attack vessels.[49] (Jakarta actually acquired the destroyer from the United States in January 1973 through the American military assistance program.) It should also be noted that Thailand opposes the Indonesian-Philippine archipelago concept because its ports on the Gulf of Thailand service ships which must use the eastern sea route.[50]

The freedom of the seas controversy, as with most international issues, has become part of the Sino-Soviet dispute. As a waxing seapower, the U.S.S.R. has opposed both the nationalization of world straits and the 200-mile coastal exploitation limit. As a self-identified spokesman for small-state interests, Peking insists that the 200-mile limit is essential to protect littoral states from having their mineral-rich underwater coastal zones mined of their resources by the big powers with no compensation. Additional reasons for China's support of the 200-mile zone include its potential for disrupting close-in operations of the growing Soviet Navy and the fact that such a zone would provide China with the opportunity to claim a sizeable portion of the wealth of the East China and Yellow seas. It has been on these grounds, for example, that Peking has objected to a Japanese-South Korean agreement to exploit undersea oil reserves off the South Korean coast. Similarly, Peking favors national control of the world's straits out of concern over Russia's military intentions:

> Everyone understands that straits within the territorial waters of littoral countries, although regularly used for international navigation cannot be changed into open seas. To put it bluntly . . . Soviet revisionism is attempting to exploit the straits . . . as open seas so that its warships and aircraft can pass through them at will and pose a threat to the peace and security of those countries.[51]

---

[47] Author's interviews in Singapore, June 1973.
[48] See the AFP (Hong Kong) accounts of 2 and 14 November 1973.
[49] AFP (Hong Kong), 27 August 1973.
[50] *The Nation*, editorial, 6 September 1973.
[51] NCNA, 9 April 1974.

The Soviets have responded to this Chinese riposte by insisting that the acceptance of a 200-mile coastal limit and the nationalization of straits would create "chaos . . . in determining the limits of territorial waters," a situation which "would lead to international friction and ultimately to international conflict." Soviet writers point to the world atlas published in China in 1972 in which "the whole of the South China Sea is shown as Chinese territorial waters. . . . The territorial waters of the Spratleys extend to the areas near the coasts of Kalimantan Island and the Philippine island of Palawan." [52]

The issues discussed in this section were all under consideration at the 1974 Law of the Sea Conference. One close observer of that conference explained an American attempt to compromise the 200-mile limit controversy by proposing a draft treaty which would create an international authority to exploit seabed resources and distribute derived income to all developing states. The latter have not bought the idea, however, suggesting they are interested less in immediate income than in direct participation in and control of offshore resources. The American interest in the compromise was less economic than strategic. As in the case of the Soviet Union, the absence of a 200-mile coastal zone would permit U.S. nuclear submarines to travel unimpeded. According to Professor Edward Miles, the United States may well trade off an agreement to the 200-mile economic zone in exchange for an agreement on free passage through the world's straits. Miles expects, however, that neither the U.S.S.R. nor Japan would be willing to ratify such an arrangement because of their fisheries' practices which have led to heavy depletion of fish off the African coast and the American West Coast. [53]

The major international oil companies do not appear to oppose the 200-mile zone. They could then negotiate licensing and shore agreements with each separate jurisdiction. If such a zone were adopted as international law and practice (which Miles believes to be unlikely because of major power refusal), the practical effect would probably be a payment of higher license fees by developed countries to developing states and contracts for joint exploitation between these states. The equity of these projected arrangements would depend on the relative bargaining capabilities of the partners.

---

[52] *New Times* (Moscow) (4), 1 February 1974.

[53] Lecture by Professor Edward Miles of the Harvard Center for International Affairs at the University of Kentucky, 31 January 1974.

3
PROSPECTS FOR NEUTRALIZATION

It is easy to understand that the choice between neutrality and alignment affects the most essential issues in any state: the decision-making process within the government; the choice of the way of development; the political, economic, and social priorities; the nature and structure of political institutions, the role of the army, police, and intelligence services within the state; the independence of foreign policy and of foreign trade. The reality of national independence is to be appreciated primarily on these grounds.

Philippe Devillers

Having examined up to this point the contemporary foreign policy environment in Asia as well as some of the obstacles to regional cooperation, this study now turns to its central question: the feasibility of neutralization as a *regional* posture for the remainder of the 1970s. The past twenty years could well be termed the era of regional alignment and polarization as Asian international politics took on the coloration of its global counterpart. Those states claiming nonaligned status in that period were only nominally unaligned (Sukarno's Indonesia), of only marginal interest to one of the poles (Burma), or large and stable enough so that neither pole believed that instability could bring about the disintegration of an independent government (India).

Part of the attractiveness of a nonalignment policy is that it grants status to those governments which do not choose to follow the hierarchical approach of alliance arrangements in which they can play only a subordinate role to extraregional powers. That is, in the 1950s and 1960s, alliances, no matter how benevolent, came to be viewed by both domestic elites in the host country and international public opinion as somehow compromising one's independence. By the 1970s, as external pressures to sustain alliance commitments diminished with the Sino-U.S. and U.S.-Soviet détentes, along with the British reduction of its East of Suez forces, Asia's national leaders could reexamine their options for the first time in twenty years.

Neutralization could provide a way of decoupling any country's security problems from the global policies of an external mentor, thus permitting the small state to focus its energy and attention on the immediate environment rather than its small role within a large framework. This projected disconnection between regional and global security matters would in turn presumably reassure the major powers that Asian affairs would not be structured by an outside rival against them. In other words, neutralization would offer security through the polar opposite of the policy of competitive alignment pursued since the mid-1950s. Instead of the great powers attempting to achieve preemptive influence in a given state's foreign policy, they would follow policies of mutual self-abnegation. Such policies would serve to reassure potential adversaries against hostile intentions.

Although the foregoing explanation appears theoretically feasible, the practical question remains of whether and how Asia can move from a situation of competitive alignment to neutralization, especially since the five ASEAN states, publicly in the vanguard of this movement, are by no means current examples of the policy they advocate. All the ASEAN states are, in fact, anti-Communist, and, with the exception of Indonesia, all are currently tied to either the United States or the ANZUK countries.

At the time of writing (spring 1975), no agreement had been reached by the ASEAN states on how neutralization was to be defined. Consensus did exist on certain conditions which would have to prevail in order for it to succeed, no matter how it would be finally defined. These conditions included: (1) an acceptance of neutralization as a regional posture by both those states adhering to it and external powers which have been active in the region; and (2) a termination of the Indochina war.[1]

Conceptual Disagreement over the Meaning of Neutralization

The November 1971 Malaysian neutralization proposal was designed to seize the initiative for restructuring regional relationships from

---

[1] These minimal preconditions for neutralization were presented in a panel discussion by the embassies of the ASEAN states at the Association for Asian Studies annual meeting in Boston, 1 April 1974.

the great powers and to head off the possible establishment of new spheres of great power influence in the wake of Nixon's forthcoming visit to China. The idea itself had been bandied about by Malaysia as early as 1968 but had run up against a number of still unresolved questions, the foremost of which concerned whether neutralization meant a formal guarantee by major external powers or merely their recognition of the new status? A second question was whether neutralization would be best served by a balance of major power activities within the region or the exclusion of such activities from it?

While no consensus has yet been reached on a working definition of neutralization, there is agreement at least on the following points: Neutralization can come about only through international agreements rather than unilateral declarations. Neutralization must be recognized by both the states accepting that status and those *guaranteeing* it. Neutralized states are obligated to refrain from certain acts, such as permitting other states to use their territory for military purposes. Guarantor states must refrain from coercing neutralized states through, for example, supporting domestic revolutionaries in the territory of the former. And, finally, neutralized states can ask for security assistance only from guarantor states if the status of the former is violated, but, in event of civil war, neutralized states must not invite foreign powers to aid in suppressing domestic rebels.[2]

The purpose of neutralization, of course, is to avoid armed international conflict. Its workability depends on the congruence of objectives among the guarantor states *inter se* and vis-à-vis the neutralized states. And the congruence of objectives can only be determined by answering some hard questions. Is there a homogeneity of interests among the states to be neutralized? Does each of the states regard its independence and national welfare to be in jeopardy? Does each of the states perceive itself as a bone of contention among outside powers?

Although the ASEAN foreign ministers have met several times since the November 1971 declaration to discuss the manner in which it might be implemented, there has been no attempt as yet to approach potential guarantor states, and all five signatories have made it clear that they would retain present security arrangements until the neutralization proposal became a reality. None of the great powers has expressed official support for the declaration, although Peking has reportedly conveyed private approval. And none of the great

---

[2] There is an excellent discussion of both the legal and political aspects of neutralization in an unpublished paper by Professor T. T. B. Koh of the University of Singapore, "The Neutralization of Southeast Asia," January 1972 (mimeo.).

powers has had anything to say about eschewing intervention in the region.

This last point has brought about an issue particularly difficult to resolve: would neutralization best be served by the exclusion of great-power activities from "the zone of peace, freedom, and neutrality," or would it be more realistic to invite all the great powers into the region in a kind of competitive balance? Nor has agreement been reached on whether and how the major powers could serve as guarantors. Malaysia, for example, seems to have recently taken the position that the major powers should *not* guarantee the neutralization effort, because that would provide them with an implied right to intervene if the process proved unworkable.[3] Malaysia's goal, then, appears to be an overall reduction in the presence and military activities of all great powers in Southeast Asia.

Singapore, by contrast, has taken the opposite view, comparable to its disagreement with Malaysia and Indonesia over the internationalization of the Malacca Straits. Singapore has followed the credo that there is safety in numbers. The more powers with a stake in Singapore, so the official thinking goes, the safer the republic will be both from single-power domination and from unfriendly neighbors. If, for example, the U.S.S.R. and China can increase their commercial ties with the region, they will have a smaller incentive to support regional insurgents.[4] Singapore officials go on to argue that it is unrealistic and futile to attempt to exclude major-power access to Southeast Asia. They will continue to operate in the region for a variety of purposes, including the Soviet-U.S. strategic relationship, the competitive diplomatic aspects of the Sino-Soviet dispute, and Japan's need for the region's material resources.[5]

There are also hard economic reasons for Singapore's multiple access posture. The People's Action party government has expanded the city-state's economy from exclusive dependence on entrepôt trade to that of a major manufacturing exporter and the primary bunkering and petroleum refinery location in Southeast Asia, with the third largest capacity in the world (after Houston and Rotterdam). But the maintenance of such an industrial complex requires the assured continuation of economic ties to the major powers, most of whom are also major investors in and major markets for Singapore.

---

[3] Presentation by Malaysian Ambassador Mohamed Khir Johari at the Association for Asian Studies, Boston, 1 April 1974.

[4] Presentation by Singapore's ambassador, ibid.

[5] Author's interviews in Singapore, June 1973.

Finally, it should be noted that Singapore is not the only member of ASEAN which supports a multiple access approach to neutralization, although it is the most outspoken. Indonesia may also desire some variation of this policy as, for example, the retention of the Seventh Fleet in Southeast Asian waters to balance the Soviet naval presence, particularly since the regional fleets are so weak. It should be added, however, that the maintenance of a naval presence does not imply support for continued base rights. The latter are increasingly viewed as provocative to other major powers, leading them to press for comparable rights in the region.[6]

Implications of the Neutralization Proposal for the ASEAN Region

The Security Dimension. The idea of Southeast Asia's neutralization is not especially new. It can be traced back, in fact, to Anthony Eden's Locarno-type proposal at the 1954 Geneva Conference on Indochina, at which he proposed a neutral belt of states which would serve to safeguard great-power interests. At that time, however, American leaders viewed neutralism as just one step short of allying with the adversary, so John Foster Dulles chose the opposite strategy of competitive alignment.

The combination of American disillusion in Indochina and British balance-of-payments difficulties has led to a retreat from the Dulles competitive alignment strategy. Asian leaders perceived this change in the aftermath of Nixon's July 1969 Guam statement, and the most significant response has been the 1971 Malaysia neutralization proposal. It is important to understand the proposal as a functional equivalent to the competitive alignment posture of the previous fifteen-to-twenty years. That is, it is designed to provide security through self-abnegation rather than association with outsiders. Neutralization, from the ASEAN states' perspective, would serve to insulate the region from Communist pressures, just as alignment was supposed to have done in the previous period.[7]

In practice, however, implementation of the neutralization proposal has been deferred if not postponed for several reasons. Foremost among them was the "chicken-egg" situation inherent in the fact that neither the U.S.S.R. nor China could be expected to become guarantors while U.S. bases remained in the region. But neither

---

[6] Author's interview with Dr. Lie Tek-jeng, National Institute for Cultural Studies, Indonesian Institute of Sciences, Jakarta, 1 June 1973.

[7] Author's interviews in Kuala Lumpur, June 1973.

Thailand nor the Philippines was prepared to jettison their American defense commitments while they were engaged in struggles with what they claimed to be externally backed insurgents. Singapore is skeptical of the proposal because of its concern that neutralization could restrict its foreign policy options as a globally oriented city-state. And Indonesia may view the prospect of neutralization as too confining a foreign-policy posture for a country with its regional potential (although a region in which external influence was circumscribed could well provide Indonesia with greater status).[8]

Indonesia's appeal for national resilience as a prerequisite for neutralization may be Jakarta's way of saying national stability should precede regional security endeavors of even a passive nature. Kuala Lumpur has responded to these doubts by stressing the long-range character of the proposal and by urging all ASEAN members to make a concerted effort to get the great powers to redefine their role and reduce their military presence in the region.[9] An initial step in this direction was taken at the July 1972 ASEAN meeting in Kuala Lumpur, where a definition of neutralization was reached, providing that the states

> shall undertake to maintain their impartiality and shall refrain from involvement directly or indirectly in ideological, political, economic, armed or other forms of conflict, particularly between powers outside the zone, and that outside powers shall not interfere in the domestic or regional affairs of the zonal states.[10]

The ambiguity of the above statement is obvious, however. Should foreign military bases be classified as interference when they exist at the express invitation of the host government? Is massive economic investment by an outside power also interference even though sought by the host state? There are no clear-cut answers to these questions. They illustrate the difficulty of moving away from a posture of outside dependence in both military and economic matters toward regional cooperation and self-reliance.

The Malaysians in particular insist that there is no viable regional alternative to neutralization *in the long run*. The United States will not become involved again in Asian land wars, and the British-Australian-New Zealand guarantees to Malaysia and Singapore are

---

[8] T. B. B. Koh and Lau Teak Soon, "Problems and Prospects of Regional Cooperation in Southeast Asia" (University of Singapore, mimeo., n.d.).

[9] Girling, "A Neutral Southeast Asia?" p. 126.

[10] Ibid., p. 125.

clearly inferior in nature. If Western alliance arrangements are disintegrating in any case, then the diplomatic problem facing the Southeast Asian states is one of disengaging without a loss of security and in insuring that the major Communist states do not have the opportunity to move in as the Western powers exit.[11] If the countries of the region promise not to become involved in the conflicts and rivalries of the major powers, they hope, in return, that the major powers will leave the region to its own devices. Such hopes may be ill-founded, however, if the major powers already possess economic and political positions they are unwilling to leave. Thus, Singapore has argued, a competitive balance of outsiders is practicable and therefore preferable to a policy of exclusion which cannot be enforced and could serve to encourage covert intervention by outside powers wishing to preempt their rivals.[12]

There are other objections to the abrogation of current military arrangements. One Philippine military officer pointed to the added drain on already strained government budgets which would follow domestic military build-ups after Western base withdrawals.[13] When queried about the possibility of regional military cooperation and the sharing of security tasks, the officer as well as respondents in all other ASEAN capitals belittled such prospects by pointing to the conflicts and mutual suspicions which still characterize the relations of the ASEAN partners. Can you imagine, he asked incredulously, the Philippines inviting in a Malaysian task force to assist in policing the Sulu Islands, or for that matter, the Malaysians requesting joint Filipino patrols against insurgents in Sabah? Similar concern would greet Malaysian forces in Singapore and Indonesian forces almost anywhere in the region.

Clearly, indigenous regional military arrangements remain limited. Since their 1965 breakup, Singapore and Malaysia maintain only an integrated air-defense system. Each prefers the presence of a small commonwealth contingent to the stationing of its neighbor's forces on its soil.[14] For some time, Malaysia has conducted joint border control operations with Thailand in the west and Indonesia in the east against Communist insurgents. Although they have been for

---

[11] Author's interviews in Kuala Lumpur, June 1973.

[12] Author's interviews in Singapore, May-June 1973; and K. K. Nair, "The Shifting Power Alignment in the Indian Ocean," in *Issues for the Seventies*, pp. 34–36.

[13] Author's interview in Manila, May 1973.

[14] See the discussion by Frank H. H. King, "The Foreign Policy of Singapore" in R. P. Barston, ed., *The Other Powers: Studies in the Foreign Policies of Small States* (London: Allen and Unwin, 1973).

the most part successful in confining insurgent activities, none of the three has expressed interest in broader military cooperation.

More than any other regional leader, Singapore's Lee Kwan Yew has been the most outspoken in urging the retention of a U.S. military presence in Asia. Sometimes to the consternation of his ASEAN colleagues, particularly in Bangkok, Lee has insisted that the Americans continue to back Thailand as a buffer against Vietminh southward expansion after U.S. military withdrawal from Indochina. Lee remains an unabashed adherent to the domino theory and continues to view North Vietnam's intentions as predatory.[15]

One recent study found that despite their government's well-known support for neutralization, even Indonesian foreign-policy and academic elites believe that the superpowers *should* continue to balance one another in Southeast Asia. Implied by the policy preference is the strong belief that because of regional military weakness and instability, Southeast Asian affairs will not be controlled by the region's members for a long time to come.[16]

Official Thai sources have repeatedly stressed that once the Indochina hostilities ceased, Bangkok would ask the Americans to withdraw their military personnel.[17] Thailand has also tightened its control over the military activities which may be prosecuted from its bases. Partly as an earnest of Thailand's good intentions toward the D.R.V. and as a reflection of its growing belief that the United States was disengaging from the Indochina war, Foreign Minister Charunphan stated that in early 1974 the United States would have to obtain permission from the Thai government if it wished to bomb Indochina from Thai bases in the future.[18]

As mentioned briefly above, China is the only major power that has expressed support for the neutralization proposal as of mid-1974. And of the major powers only China had no substantial economic or military presence in the region to protect. Neutralization in Southeast Asia could generate two advantages for the P.R.C.: it could block Soviet attempts at alliance-building under the guise of Asian collective security, and it would increase regional pressure on the United States to withdraw its bases from the region. As David

---

15 See the interviews with Lee Kwan Yew in *The Mirror* (Singapore), 6 November 1972 and 29 January 1973.

16 Donald G. McCloud, *Indonesian Foreign Policy in Southeast Asia: A Study of Patterns of Behavior* (Unpublished Ph.D. dissertation, University of South Carolina, 1974), pp. 29–30.

17 Typical is the interview with Deputy Foreign Minister Chatchai in *The Nation*, 1 February 1973.

18 *The World* (Bangkok), 23 February 1974.

Mozingo points out, great-power disengagement would also fit Peking's claim that it will not behave as a great power seeking a sphere of influence.[19] The claim covers necessity with a cloak of virtue, of course, since China does not possess the capability to play the game of military balance as do the United States and the Soviet Union.

Finally, it should be briefly mentioned that Thailand, whose primary orientation is toward mainland Southeast Asia, has been urging either ASEAN's expansion to include the four countries of Indochina and Burma or the creation of a new group of ten to discuss the neutralization of *all* Southeast Asia.[20] Bangkok's needs differ from those of its insular colleagues, for it is the only government facing an insurgency directly backed by North Vietnam—hence, the desire to obtain Hanoi's commitment to neutralization. The prospect of such an agreement appears extremely dim, however. Hanoi has expressed no interest in the ASEAN proposal, and it has never tried to hide its membership in and alliance with the socialist camp. On the contrary, the D.R.V. needed alliances to obtain the military wherewithal to continue its struggle throughout Indochina. Although Hanoi has not objected to the Kuala Lumpur proposal, when it mentions neutrality in Southeast Asia, it carefully excludes itself. Neutralism is supported, rather, as a means of encouraging Western-oriented states to loosen their ties with Washington and London.[21]

The Economic Dimension. Security ties are not the only links with outsiders which would be affected by an effort to neutralize Southeast Asia. Economic associations with external powers could also be altered, especially if they were viewed as creating an inordinate degree of dependence. That is, if foreign investors come to control important sectors of regional economies, say, rubber and tin in Malaysia, is it realistic to believe that the governments can be neutral or that their foreign investors would not exercise political influence to protect their positions? Put another way, would political independence prevail if the mineral and industrial sectors of the economy were mortgaged to outsiders?

---

[19] David M. Mozingo, "China's Future Role in Southeast Asia," in Soon, ed., *New Directions*, pp. 45–47.

[20] See the open letter to Pathet Lao leader, Prince Souphanouvang, in *The Nation*, 10 April 1974.

[21] See the perceptive discussion in Nguyen Manh Hung, "The Two Vietnams and the Proposal for a Neutralized Southeast Asia," in Soon, ed., *New Directions*, pp. 138–144.

Yet it is equally clear that the Asian states cannot reduce their dependence on outside investment without severely curtailing their modernization plans. Current projections indicate that an annual GNP growth rate of 6 percent will not even provide enough new jobs for the growth in the labor force of developing countries in this decade.[22] The most likely way to accelerate the growth of GNP is through capital importation. But the ability of developing states to attract investment, except for raw material exploitation, is limited by the discriminatory practices of industrialized countries against the import of labor-intensive manufactured goods.[23]

Although the ASEAN states have been characterized as "outward looking" and "innovative" with respect to the creation of new regional institutions to promote sectoral integration and trade liberalization, success might still be only marginally related to the needs of the countries. Hiroshi Kitamura, former director of research and planning for ECAFE, has shown that intraregional trade will remain limited in Southeast Asia because of a lack of supply and demand among the region's members. Thus, in the 1960s, globally, intraregional trade for most countries came to about 20 percent of their world trade. But for the ASEAN states, the figure was only 10 percent.[24] Moreover, the fact that all ASEAN states with the exception of Singapore possess underdeveloped economies means that they are competitors for foreign aid and investment rather than partners. Indeed, even ASEAN cooperation can drain scarce resources from one country to another, as was demonstrated in 1973 when Indonesian teachers were attracted by the higher salaries available in Malaysia.[25]

The foregoing discussion illustrates an endemic problem for most developing countries: an unwillingness to subordinate immediate national advantages to long-term economic gains. The ASEAN states' behavior during the 1973 energy crisis, induced by the Arab boycott and OAPEC price increases, provides an even more dramatic example. Thailand, Singapore, and the Philippines all depend on the Middle East for oil, but when their economies were threatened by

---

[22] Edward Fried, "Foreign Economic Policy: The Search for a Strategy," in Henry Owen, ed., *The Next Phase*, p. 189.

[23] Ibid., pp. 190–191.

[24] See Seiji Naya and Richard Schatz, "Trade, Investment, and Aid," and Bernard K. Gordon, "Rhetoric and Reality in Regional Cooperation," in Harald Malmgren, ed., *Pacific Basin Development: The American Interests* (Lexington, Mass.: D. C. Heath, 1972), pp. 77, 83–84.

[25] Author's interview with Dr. Lie Tek-jeng, National Institute for Cultural Studies, Jakarta, 1 June 1973.

the Arab cutbacks, neither Indonesia nor Malaysia, the two oil-producers of the group, would help. Indonesia's major markets are Japan, which takes over 70 percent of Jakarta's petroleum exports, and the United States. Malaysia sells most of its production outside the ASEAN area in exchange for hard currency. In November 1973, the Philippines proposed that ASEAN adopt a common oil policy under which oil-producers would help nonproducers. Neither Indonesia nor Malaysia expressed interest in the proposal.[26]

A somewhat comparable problem confronts any attempt within ASEAN to develop a coordinated regional policy toward external investors. National conditions vary so greatly that one capital may wish to apply stringent controls to external investors, for example, Bangkok's concern over Japanese economic control of its industry, while another capital may welcome such investors both because they provide for development and, as in Manila's case, offer some leverage against the dominant American position in the economy. In Jakarta and Kuala Lumpur, external investors may serve the additional function of diluting indigenous Chinese control of the local economies.[27]

In any event, there is scant evidence to suggest that the role of foreign investment will diminish in Southeast Asia over the next several years. In Malaysia, for example, almost 70 percent of the country's investment capital is owned by foreigners.[28] Singapore's economic orientation is predominantly extraregional; its regional contribution has been confined primarily to the provision of financial services and technology for urbanization, transportation, and light industry, which has resulted in its becoming the sixth largest foreign investor in Indonesia.[29] In the Philippines, U.S. military spending is a primary source of foreign exchange; base-related spending in 1972 totaled $158 million. Additionally over 50,000 Filipinos are employed at the Clark and Subic Bay bases.[30]

Perhaps the most significant example of Southeast Asia's continued economic dependence on the West, even as military relations are weakened, is Indonesia. Officially nonaligned and viewed by many as the "natural" leader of ASEAN, Indonesia has relied since 1967

---

[26] See the background discussion in the *New York Times*, 27 January 1974.

[27] Author's discussion with the staff of the Center for Asian Studies, University of the Philippines, 23 May 1973.

[28] Hamlin Robinson, "The Multinational Corporation in Perspective," in *Issues for the Seventies*, p. 58.

[29] Marvin Rogers, "Malaysia and Singapore," *Asian Survey*, vol. 12, no. 2 (February 1972); and author's interview with Professor T. T. B. Koh, Faculty of Law, University of Singapore, 6 June 1973.

[30] Information supplied by the U.S. Embassy, Manila, May 1973.

on foreign capital for some 80 percent of its developmental investment. By 1973, the Inter-Governmental Group on Indonesia (IGGI)—a Western consortium of states created to coordinate governmental assistance to Jakarta after Sukarno's overthrow—provided some $760 million annually. The projection for 1974 went up to $876 million.[31]

Indonesia's economic success over the past several years, enhanced by the rise in petroleum prices since 1973, has created new political problems, however. Beginning in 1971, a low-key concern began over alleged development of American-controlled institutional influence over the Indonesian economy and its foreign policy. The technocrats, responsible for Jakarta's economic plans, were accused of being unduly subservient to the World Bank. Their American educational credentials were stigmatized in the press which referred to them collectively as the "Berkeley Mafia." In effect, two of the country's national goals appeared to be running afoul of one another: economic development, which required foreign aid and a relatively heavy emphasis on the modern, industrial, urban sector of the economy, and nonalignment, which would seem to require a reduction in foreign dependence. Also associated with the latter was an economic complaint that Indonesia's planners should concern themselves more with distributive justice than with capital accumulation.[32] For Indonesia, the old questions have presented themselves once more: can there be development without foreign aid, and can there be foreign aid without some kind of external influence on domestic policy decisions? The answer to both would appear to be no. But the starkness of the dichotomy may be misleading. The real issue is probably less that of foreign aid versus political independence than one of how much foreign involvement in a nation's economy must occur before the reins of control are transferred outside the country? The answer to this question will vary with the strength of a given country's political institutions, the diversity of its economy, and the political organization behind the foreign investment. Southeast Asia's diversity, of course, implies no single answer.

The Neutralization Proposal and Southeast Asia's Political Order.

One of the purposes of neutralization is to prevent a political Balkanization of Southeast Asia that could attend a new scramble for alliance

---

[31] Robert C. Horn, "Indonesia's Response to Changing Big Power Alignments," *Pacific Affairs*, vol. 46, no. 4 (Winter 1973-74), p. 517; and the *Far Eastern Economic Review*, 24 December 1973, p. 20.

[32] *Far Eastern Economic Review*, 25 February 1974, p. 13.

as the Western powers disengage. The Thai suggestion that ASEAN membership be broadened to include all of mainland Southeast Asia is designed to extend the sphere of neutrality and hence add to the region's security.[33] The prospect of additional membership has not been greeted enthusiastically by the other ASEAN states, however, both because of the political instability of Indochina and the desire to avoid any direct association with Communist governments. The most likely prospective addition would be Burma, but Ne Win has shown little desire to affiliate, stipulating that Burma could not join ASEAN until all U.S. bases were withdrawn from Thailand and all members had recognized Peking.[34] In short, Burma would make no move until the Indochina conflict had fully terminated.

The tentativeness of ASEAN political moves reflects the youth and inexperience of regional cooperation in Southeast Asia and the fact that mutual trust takes careful nurturing. Indeed, until mid-1973, some of the ASEAN heads-of-state had still not met one another. Although regular consultation occurs at the foreign ministers level and below, it is still premature to speak of any ASEAN *system.*

If ASEAN follows the path of other third world regional organizations (for example, the Organizations of American States and African Unity), then suspicion toward the larger by the smaller states will inhibit the creation of a regional system with political institutions capable of settling member disputes. Rather, the regional organization serves as a forum for relating member interests to outsiders, as ASEAN has currently attempted organization-wide approaches to the EEC. ASEAN has also provided a mantle of mutual support against possible outside intervention in regional conflicts. Thus, both Indonesia and Malaysia supported the Philippines against allegations of Muslim suppression at the 1973 Muslim Conference in Libya.

Nevertheless, for the organization to prosper, each state must be able to derive some benefits through collective action which would presumably be unavailable if sought through its single foreign policy. For a core power, such as Indonesia, ASEAN served both to reintegrate it into regional politics and to provide a constructive framework for national assertiveness. In the past few years, Jakarta's national ambitions have been demonstrated through its membership on the United Nations Security Council, the presidency of the General Assembly, membership on the Vietnam ceasefire international control commission, convocation of the Asian Conference on Cambodia, the

---

[33] Speech by Foreign Minister Charunphan in *The Nation,* 17 January 1974.
[34] *Far Eastern Economic Review,* 11 March 1974, p. 24.

executive secretaryship of ECAFE, and its provision of a location for the new ASEAN permanent secretariat. Indonesian analysts themselves point to ASEAN as one means of excluding the superpowers from intervening militarily in regional affairs, though they do not see it as inhibiting a continued superpower presence.[35]

In a recent survey of approximately one hundred respondents, broadly classified as members of the Indonesian foreign policy elite (middle level government officials, journalists, and academics), 72 percent believed that Indonesia would become the dominant power within ASEAN. And they went on to counterpose Indonesia's position in insular Southeast Asia to North Vietnam's on the mainland.[36] As McCloud points out, however, there may still be considerable suspicion among Indonesia's ASEAN partners over the longevity of its current cooperative demeanor:

> Within the region of Southeast Asia, Indonesia's foreign policy has varied considerably over time. There is a common presumption (both academic and popular) that Indonesia is destined to play a leading role in the region. Justifications for this role range from the vast relative size of Indonesia and her supposed natural wealth to her great cultural heritage to her long bloody struggle for independence. However, through most of Indonesia's period as an independent state, her regional policies have varied from condescending to open hostility and animosity. Only in the early 1950s and again under the New Order has Indonesia proved the stability and evenness toward other regional states that would allow her to play a significant leadership role in the region.[37]

And, as McCloud goes on to demonstrate through an empirical events-data analysis of Indonesia's interactions with Southeast Asia, the amount of attention given by Jakarta to ASEAN has been on the decline in the 1970s. Moreover, most of the attention was of a verbal rather than an action character through 1973.[38] The implications of these findings for an Indonesian leadership role in ASEAN are somewhat disquieting, particularly since they deviate so markedly from

---

[35] See the Indonesian defense analysts cited by McCloud, *Indonesian Foreign Policy in Southeast Asia*, pp. 27–30.

[36] Ibid., p. 118. This viewpoint was independently corroborated by Professor Donald Weatherbee's interviews in Southeast Asia in the summer of 1973 as reported at the Seminar on North Vietnam and the Security of Southeast Asia, University of South Carolina, 3-5 October 1973.

[37] Ibid., p. 32.

[38] Ibid., p. 103.

analysts' interpretations and projections of Jakarta's ultimate dominance within the association. Rather, McCloud has found that Indonesia prefers to conduct its regional relations on a bilateral rather than a multilateral basis, inferring that at least for the time being, it has little confidence in ASEAN becoming a significant political actor.

This view of ASEAN's limitations can be found in other regional capitals as well. The author's own interviews reinforce the foregoing discussion in that there was virtual consensus that each state's security problems were primarily internal, its own responsibility, and not susceptible to *regional* action, although in several cases handled on a bilateral basis. Indeed, the only state that has continued to lobby for an ASEAN role in Indochina has not been Indonesia but Thailand, although it should be mentioned that Indonesia does serve as a member of the ICCS. The Thai position, of course, grows out of its desire to associate the insular-oriented ASEAN more closely with Bangkok's mainland security needs. In both 1973 and 1974, Thai officials have called for Indochinese participation at ASEAN ministerial conferences to no avail. Hanoi has bluntly refused, castigating the association as a Trojan horse for continued American intervention.

Thus, we come back to the viability of the ASEAN neutralization proposal. The most pessimistic observers argue that it is meaningless.[39] They cite how Indonesia is not really interested because neutralization is a passive status, requiring external guarantees which would too severely constrain a putative regional power like Jakarta. Thailand will remain uninterested while North Vietnam's intentions toward it and Indochina are unresolved. And Singapore has indicated many times that it prefers a competitive regional balance to neutralization. This leaves Malaysia and the Philippines as the only two ASEAN states with an apparently genuine interest in promoting neutralization, for neither aspires to regional preeminence nor is directly threatened by a powerful neighbor.

In sum, for neutralization to work, extant conflicts must be resolved *beforehand*. That is, neutralization cannot be a technique for settling current disputes but rather a way of inhibiting the development of future conflicts once current hostilities have been terminated. Neutralization could be a way of assuring the great powers (China, Japan, the United States, and the U.S.S.R.) that political alignments inimical to their continued peaceful access to the region will not occur. In return, however, they must agree to refrain from either supporting or opposing the endemic political processes which work themselves through, sometimes violently, in all developing

---

[39] Author's interviews in Singapore, June 1973.

states. (The likelihood of such policies of self-abnegation by the major powers will be discussed further in Chapter 5.)

The Soviet Alternative: "Asian Collective Security"

The Soviets have devised an alternative to the ASEAN neutralization proposal, first broached by Secretary Brezhnev in June 1969, the month before the world Communist conference. In what has generally been interpreted as a trial balloon, Brezhnev spoke of a system of collective security for Asia. Following on the heels of the border incidents with China and announcements of British and American plans for the future reduction of their forces in Asia, the proposal was seen as an anti-China gambit and a potential Soviet SEATO. Responding to these criticisms, Foreign Minister Gromyko assured the doubters that Brezhnev's concept was not directed against any particular country, nor would it take the form of a military pact.[40] The concept proved to be essentially passive and negative. It did not appear to propose the creation of a new security organization as much as a regional agreement to close the door after the projected withdrawal of the United States and Britain, thus precluding their reentry into regional political affairs. Once this has occurred, the Soviets could presumably contain Chinese activity with little difficulty.

The Soviet proposal was reactivated in March 1972, following Nixon's visit to China and the Russian conclusion of mutual friendship treaties with India and Iraq. Moscow began to publicize its 1971 Indian treaty as a prototype for other Asian countries to follow, implying that Asian collective security could be achieved through a series of bilateral arrangements with the Soviet Union.[41] Adamant Chinese opposition, however, plus the vagueness of the concept, and the desire not to replace dependence on one set of great powers with similar dependence on its adversary have virtually halted the Soviet proposal in its tracks. Only Iran and India have proferred verbal endorsement. And Mrs. Gandhi has pointedly noted on several occasions that India's treaty with the Soviet Union in no way changes its nonalignment policy.[42]

Although the foregoing is a brief analysis of the status (or perhaps lack of status) of the Russian proposal in Asia, the primary task of this section of our study is to explore the purposes behind

---

[40] *Pravda*, 11 July 1969.

[41] See the discussions in Millar, "Prospects for Regional Security," pp. 464–465, and Jean Riollet, "Asian Collective Security Revisited," *Radio Liberty Dispatch*, 20 February 1974.

[42] Riollet, "Asian Collective Security Revisited," p. 4.

and ramifications of the collective security proposal as a manifestation of the Russian goal of establishing a permanent Asian presence. These ramifications should not be viewed as entirely negative by either the Asian states or by the West. Indeed, from the perspective of a concern for regional stability, a permanent Soviet presence could provide: (1) a balance to overweening political and economic reliance on the United States, (2) more options for the states of the regions, (3) a further erosion of the belief that communism is monolithic, and (4) the possibility of Soviet willingness to cooperate in such regional endeavors as the Asian Development Bank, in which it has not yet chosen to participate.

For some time now, a doctrinal basis for Soviet collaboration with third world nationalist regimes has existed, rationalizing long-term Russian support for their development rather than mere tactical collaboration against common external foes. The concept of the "national democratic state," developed in the early 1960s and still operative, justifies Soviet support for countries which are non-Communist but appear to be taking noncapitalist developmental paths. Although originally viewed by Khrushchev as the first stage of a two-stage revolution through which the state would move toward socialism, by 1971 the CPSU took pains to assert that the noncapitalist path would probably not lead to socialism but should still be supported as a means of enhancing regional stability, weakening Western influence, and promoting détente by reducing international tension.[43]

Thus, in the course of the 1970s, the U.S.S.R. has consciously underplayed its relations with third world Communist parties, as for example, in mid-1969, when it stopped publicizing a pro-Moscow Indonesian Communist party which had come into existence a year earlier. Rather, Moscow has concentrated on establishing state-to-state ties, beginning in the last half of the 1960s when diplomatic relations were established with Malaysia and Singapore, followed soon after by a joint shipping agreement with the latter which permitted Asian exporters to move their goods at rates substantially lower than those of the conference lines. Diplomatic relations with Thailand and Indonesia have existed for some time. And most observers believe that relations will be established with the Philippines sometime in 1975, at the same time Manila recognizes Peking.[44]

---

[43] For a clear discussion of this important Soviet ideological development, see Geoffrey Jukes, *The Soviet Union in Asia* (Berkeley: University of California Press, 1973), pp. 23, 27.

[44] A good general discussion of Soviet policy in Southeast Asia may be found in Robert C. Horn, "Changing Soviet Policies and Sino-Soviet Competition in Southeast Asia," *Orbis*, vol. 17, no. 2 (Summer 1973).

Moscow's overall lack of interest in Asian Communist parties reflects their generally peripheral role in the domestic politics of their respective countries and the fact that most have been oriented toward Peking. As the Soviet ambassador to Singapore reportedly remarked in late 1970, "he doubted whether the Communists in Indonesia, Malaysia, or Thailand followed real scientific Marxism." [45]

Beginning in 1970, the U.S.S.R. reconsidered its hostile attitude toward Indonesia, despite its continued depredations against the PKI, its heavy reliance on Western investment, and the recrudescence of private-enterprise capitalism. Moscow offered to sell spare parts for Indonesia's Russian-supplied military equipment and agreed to postpone the country's huge Soviet debt repayment of well over $1 billion. At the same time, the U.S.S.R. offered new aid to other non-Communist Asian states. With the exception of India, however, no non-Communist Asian state has chosen to become heavily dependent on Soviet support, suggesting a continued wariness about Soviet political intentions and also perhaps a lack of confidence in the quality of their materials. For example, in 1972 Burma sought only $240,000 in aid from Russia, as compared with over $5 million from the United States and over $20 million from Japan.[46] India's military establishment, however, appears to be relying heavily for its modernization on both the indigenous manufacture of Soviet-designed equipment under license and its direct importation. The Russians have reportedly supplied India with some of its most up-to-date equipment, including SAM-6 missiles, which were used so effectively by the Egyptians in the 1973 October War.[47]

An additional explanation for the Russian Asian collective security proposal is the rationale it provides for a growing naval presence in the Pacific–Indian Ocean region. Maintained at the relatively modest level of twenty to twenty-five vessels in the Indian Ocean, the Soviet naval contingent from its Pacific fleet serves several purposes. Strategically, it is the opening phase of a process designed to connect Russia's eastern and western fleets for the first time in the country's history; the vast Russian continent's inland seas do not

---

[45] *The Hindu* (Delhi), 22 November 1970, cited in Jukes, *The Soviet Union in Asia*, p. 145.

[46] Horn, "Changing Soviet Policies," p. 508. See also Jukes, *The Soviet Union in Asia*, pp. 253–260, who points out that U.S. aid utilized in non-Communist Asia through most of the 1960s was ten times the Soviet figure.

[47] Reuters (London), 3 January 1974. For a general discussion of the growing Indian dependence on Russian military supplies, see Stephen P. Cohen, "South Asia: Security and Defense Factors" (a paper presented to the Association for Asian Studies, Boston, April 1974).

provide such an opportunity. When the Suez Canal is reopened, the Soviet Navy will be able to transit its 38-foot depth, but ships of the *Forrestal* and *Enterprise* classes, the main U.S. strike carriers, will not.[48] A permanent Indian Ocean presence is also part of the Soviet Union's "new navy" with a blue-water role, not only in Asia but throughout the world, showing the flag and escorting the country's rapidly expanding merchant fleet. An enhanced naval presence in the Pacific and Indian Oceans also serves to monitor the activities of American nuclear submarines and to keep watch on any Chinese naval action as it develops in the next several years. And the presence of a Russian navy may serve to influence local governments and possibly deter U.S. action.

The inception of a Russian deep-water navy may be traced back to the 1962 Cuban missile crisis, when it was demonstrated that strategic nuclear power was not sufficient to attain a number of U.S.S.R. foreign policy goals against American conventional-force superiority. American control of the oceans at that time demonstrated the difficulties of an inferior naval power such as the Soviet Union. Even with its impressive modernization program of the 1960s and 1970s which, according to one analyst, has led the U.S.S.R. to "the world's largest and most modern surface navy" as well as to the world's largest submarine fleet, closer examination reveals a number of major gaps in Russian naval development and gives credence to the interpretation of the Soviet Navy's role as still being one of coastal defense and the interdiction of enemy surface vessels and submarines rather than the projection of Soviet military power to distant lands.[49]

Because the eastern and western exits from the Soviet Union force Russian ships to pass through foreign-controlled waters in the North Sea and the Sea of Japan, the Soviet Navy operates under a considerable strategic disadvantage as compared with the United States Navy, whose worldwide base network facilitates the transfer of major units from one fleet to another and whose ships transit waters controlled for the most part by either the United States or its allies.[50]

The Soviet Navy's ability to project and sustain its presence in a hostile environment remains modest. Its marine corps is estimated

---

[48] R. M. Burrell and Alvin J. Cottrell, *Iran, the Arabian Peninsula, and the Indian Ocean* (New York: National Strategy Information Center, 1972), p. 35.
[49] Norman Polmar, *Soviet Naval Power: Challenge for the 1970's* (New York: National Strategy Information Center, 1972), pp. 1, 34.
[50] Jukes, *The Soviet Union in Asia*, p. 76.

at only 15,000 troops. It has no capability to deploy fixed-wing aircraft on naval vessels, or to supply air cover for amphibious landings or sea-based air power to client regimes. Nor is there any evidence, despite press reports, that the U.S.S.R. has acquired permanent base rights anywhere on the Asian littoral.[51] The Soviet use of ports in neutral countries should not be confused with base rights, for access to the former can be withdrawn at any time. Moreover, neutral ports cannot provide the security necessary for the repair of secret equipment or the storage of ammunition. The conclusion that the U.S.S.R. has no safe base facilities in the western Pacific or the Indian Ocean is buttressed by the fact that its naval contingents include auxiliary supply ships, whose obvious purpose is to service the naval vessels at sea.[52]

An internal debate continues in the Soviet leadership over the role of the navy and the cost of continuing to build it up over the next decade. Naval advocates argue that the Soviet Union should acquire what Henry Kissinger has defined as "useable military power," which only the navy can provide in the new political and strategic global situation now emerging. The October 1973 Middle East War gave this naval lobby some powerful ammunition for its argument, as the Sixth Fleet took up battle stations in the Mediterranean, while the Russians had nothing comparable in the area to deter it. When the Soviets put their airborne divisions on alert, the United States responded with a global alert which, Soviet naval advocates might well have argued, demonstrated that Soviet behavior was provocative and tension-inducing. If, on the other hand, the Russians possessed a battle-ready naval force on the scene, its effect would have been far less provocative—just as the United States considered the movement of the Sixth Fleet innocent of any provocative intent.[53]

The United States Navy and the Soviet Union may be on the verge of a competitive naval development race in the Indian Ocean. At least the littoral states fear so. Each naval power believes the other is intent upon establishing permanent base facilities designed, in part, to increase the difficulty of the other's operation. According to the Australian strategist T. B. Millar, the Soviet presence in the Indian Ocean is designed to achieve: "(a) influence over both ends of the Suez-Red Sea passage; (b) the replacement of Great Britain as the dominant external power in the Persian Gulf, placing Western

[51] Blechman, *The Changing Soviet Navy*, pp. 25, 30.

[52] Jukes, *The Soviet Union in Asia*, pp. 80–81.

[53] See the discussion by Victor Zorza in "The Kremlin Power Struggle: Part 4," *Radio Liberty Dispatch*, 1 February 1974, pp. 15–16.

and Japanese oil supplies in a potential hostage position; (c) the military underpinning for its Asian collective security proposal; (d) observation of American naval activities, particularly the Poseidon-class submarines; (e) access to raw materials and trade partners; and (f) positions of political influence in the littoral countries through the availability of useable force—thus interdicting America's hitherto freedom to intervene in local wars." [54] By 1972, the Soviets had exceeded American naval port-time in the region by a four-to-one ratio. [55] And as early as 1970, the number of Russian ships calling at Singapore passed the 500 mark. Because of a lack of ship repair facilities in the Soviet Far East, Singapore's former British naval dockyard and its new Japanese-financed yard at Jurong have been used to repair Russian merchant ships. [56]

The only local navy being supplied by the Soviet Union in the Indian Ocean region is India's. Between 1968 and 1972, the U.S.S.R. transferred four modern submarines (with the promise of an additional four), five escort ships, six to eight Osa missile patrol boats, and one submarine tender. And Western diplomatic sources claim that, after the Brezhnev November 1973 visit, Moscow promised over an additional $2 billion in military aid, matching the Pentagon's arms deal with Iran. [57] Nevertheless, New Delhi's naval capability remains confined to coastal defense, although it did shell and effectively disable its smaller Pakistani counterpart in the early days of the December 1971 Indo-Pakistani War.

Although the Soviet naval presence has waxed since 1968, it should be emphasized that only the United States actually possesses full-scale naval facilities in the region, both at Subic Bay in the Philippines and Sattahip in Thailand. Additionally, the United States is currently debating the wisdom of expanding its small-scale naval communications facility at Diego Garcia in the Chagos Archipelago (located in the virtual geographic center of the Indian Ocean) possibly to accommodate large aircraft and major aircraft carriers.

The possible expansion of the Diego Garcia facility has created a furor among the littoral states, almost all of which supported the joint resolution of India and Sri Lanka (Ceylon) in the United Nations General Assembly declaring the Indian Ocean a zone of peace and

[54] Cited in Burrell and Cottrell, *Iran, the Arabian Peninsula, and the Indian Ocean*, pp. 34–36.

[55] Ibid., p. 32.

[56] Jukes, *The Soviet Union in Asia*, p. 148.

[57] Polmar, *Soviet Naval Power*, p. 48; and Denzil Peiris, "The Water's Mine," *Far Eastern Economic Review*, 17 December 1973, p. 22.

freedom and asking the great powers to withdraw their military fleets. Even such normally pro-American governments as Australia, Indonesia, Thailand, Iran, and Pakistan have publicly opposed the possible establishment of a full-scale American base facility on Diego Garcia. The essential argument of the opponents of American expansion is that "if the U.S. naval establishment makes out a case on the basis of American national interest for building up base facilities and maintaining a permanent naval presence, the Soviet naval establishment will be in a much better position to put forward justification for a similar presence in the Indian Ocean." [58]

In actuality, there may be a conflict between some Soviet "big navy" advocates, who would prefer to see a modest naval competition with the United States in the Indian Ocean to strengthen their argument for service expansion, and strategic analysts within the Soviet defense establishment. For the latter, a U.S. submarine presence is more threatening than any comparable Soviet fleet projection in the Indian Ocean because of the region's geographical proximity to the U.S.S.R. In short, an agreement to withdraw from the Indian Ocean by both powers would serve Soviet ends disproportionately by removing a proximate American strategic presence. Thus, the joint declaration following Secretary Brezhnev's November 1973 visit to India expressed the Soviet Union's readiness to accept the Indian Ocean peace-zone proposal. As early as June 1971, Brezhnev had stated an interest in "limiting the cruises of navies in distant waters"; and in February 1972, U.S. officials indicated a willingness to discuss the neutralization of the Indian Ocean.[59] No progress had apparently been made by mid-1975, however. In reality, it appears highly unlikely that the Soviet Union would threaten interference with Japanese or other Western shipping in the Indian Ocean. First of all, such interference would be considered an act of war. And no war with the Western powers or Japan would *begin* with naval interference. Secondly, in retaliation Europe and Japan could readily bottle up Soviet shipping at its Baltic and Tsushima Straits exits.

Although there may have been some disagreement between the U.S. State Department and the U.S. Navy prior to the 1973 Middle

---

[58] Delhi Overseas Service in English, 14 March 1974.

[59] Jukes, *The Soviet Union in Asia*, p. 89. See also Vevendra Kaushik, *The Indian Ocean: Towards a Peace Zone* (Delhi: Vikas, 1972), p. 118. But with the commissioning of Trident submarines in the last half of the 1970s, the Indian Ocean loses its strategic nuclear value to the United States because the greater range of the Trident missile permits the U.S. Navy to target the same cities in the U.S.S.R. from the Atlantic and Pacific oceans that it may previously have targeted from the Indian Ocean.

East War on whether the United States should expand its Diego Garcia facility, it seems to have disappeared in the aftermath of the war and the oil embargo. Admiral Elmo Zumwalt appeared to be speaking for both the foreign and defense policy establishments when he testified before Congress that "events such as the Arab-Israeli War, the oil embargo, and ensuing price rises show that our interests in the Indian Ocean are directly linked with our interests in Europe and Asia, and more broadly, with our fundamental interest in maintaining a stable, world-wide balance of power. . . ."[60] Zumwalt was saying, in effect, that the American naval presence was necessary not only for strategic nuclear purposes but also to protect the sea lanes for Middle Eastern oil. This view contrasts starkly with a statement made in August 1971 before the House Foreign Affairs Committee by Ronald Spiers, director of the State Department's Bureau of Politico-Military Affairs:

> Thus far, we do consider that over the next five years our interest there [the Indian Ocean] will be of substantially lower order than those of either of the great ocean basins of the Atlantic and the Pacific . . . therefore there appear to be no requirements at this time for us to feel compelled to control or even decisively influence any part of the Indian Ocean or its littoral. Given the nature of our interest there and the current level of Soviet and Chinese involvement, we consider that on balance our present interests are served by normal commercial, political, and military access.[61]

If Zumwalt's view prevails, it seems unlikely that a naval race in the Indian Ocean can be avoided, for the United States would then possess three major regional naval complexes while the Soviet Union still relied on mooring buoys and a possible harbor at Berbera, Somalia.[62] Malaysian Prime Minister Tun Abdul Razak has characterized such a competitive Soviet-American naval race as a basic "threat" to "the realization of the Kuala Lumpur declaration for the establishment of a zone of peace, freedom and neutrality in this part of the world." Citing a recent UN panel report warning that the Diego Garcia project would almost certainly set off a Soviet search

---

[60] Weintraub, "Value of Diego Garcia." See also Joint Chiefs of Staff Chairman Admiral Moorer's statement in U.S. Congress, Senate, Committee on Armed Services, *Hearings on Military Procurements Supplemental–Fiscal Year 1974* (Washington, D. C.: U.S. Government Printing Office, 1974), pp. 40–61.

[61] Cited in Burrell and Cottrell, *Iran, the Arabian Peninsula, and the Indian Ocean*, pp. 40–41.

[62] Senate, Committee on Armed Services, *Hearings on Military Procurement*, p. 47.

for comparable base facilities, Razak pleaded for "the superpowers' guarantee of a neutral zone" in lieu of competitive deployments.[63]

An Indian Ocean neutral zone could potentially link South Asian security concerns with the ASEAN neutralization concept for Southeast Asia. But the U.S. Navy's contention that the Indian Ocean is a naval vacuum which must be filled by itself and the Soviet Navy threatens to scratch the notion before it has a chance of being seriously considered in either Moscow or Washington.[64] The arms-race dynamics involved here contain the elements of a classic paradox. Virtually all the littoral states would prefer that neither the Soviet Union nor the United States extend permanent naval operations into the Indian Ocean. But, at the same time, they agree that if one power does, so should the other. Thus, *security* will not be improved; it will simply be more costly.

The overall American development plan for Diego Garcia is estimated to cost some $75 million by the late 1970s, the bulk going for airfield development and harbor dredging, sufficient to accommodate B-52, ASW, and KC-135 tanker aircraft on the former and part of a carrier task force in the latter.[65]

Perhaps the most succinct objection to the Pentagon plans has been made by Senator Claiborne Pell:

> With the closing of the Suez Canal in 1967, the Indian Ocean advocates argued that a U.S. presence was needed because the Indian Ocean was less accessible to the U.S. forces.
>
> Now with the reopening of the canal, it is argued that a permanent U.S. presence is needed to offset a potential expansion of Soviet presence made possible by the opening of the canal. Apparently, from the Defense Department viewpoint if the canal is closed that is why we should have a presence there. And if it is opened, we should have a presence there. Whatever the circumstance, an argument has been found to justify expansion into the Indian Ocean. It is part of a defense outlook that has as its basic objective a dominant American naval presence in every warm ocean in the world, the creation of a "Mare Americanum per Munde."
>
> If we really want to dominate the oceans of the world, that follows. But if what we are after is to serve the freedom

---

[63] Kuala Lumpur International Service, 17 May 1974.

[64] See Senate, Committee on Armed Services, *Hearings on Military Procurement*, p. 46.

[65] Ibid., pp. 59–60, 63–64.

of passage of the oceans and a limitation of our own commitments around the world and hostages for future hostilities, then I would seek fewer, not more bases.[66]

Senator Pell exposed one of the fundamental ambiguities of the Nixon Doctrine insofar as it still operates in Asia in the mid-1970s: the tension between maintaining alliance commitments with "usable" (that is, naval) force and an urging upon regional states the primary responsibility for their own security. Should these states desire to opt for neutralism rather than alliance, their plans may be thwarted by both the American and Soviet conception of how great powers should balance each other in the world's major seas and oceans. As Senator Pell points out, freedom of the seas requires the opportunity for unimpeded access, not a permanent base in the Indian Ocean. No great power threatens unimpeded access. But if Soviet and American goals go beyond freedom of movement to include great-power balance and the display of naval prowess, then prospects for the neutralization of the region are very dim indeed.

India, South Asia's most prominent state, has recognized the inability of the region's members to change great-power behavior on this issue. Despite its 1971 treaty with the Soviet Union and its concomitant military reliance on Moscow, Indian officials oppose any inordinate dependence on the U.S.S.R. for New Delhi's security. The country's May 1974 test of a nuclear device was evidence of India's continued quest for the symbols of at least a regional great-power status. When, in May 1972, the U.S.S.R. still received President Nixon, despite the bombing and mining of the Hanoi-Haiphong area, Indian leaders realized the qualitative difference between their relationship with Moscow and that of the United States. Shortly thereafter, the Indian Foreign Ministry began to cultivate better relations with Australia and New Zealand and to express hopes for improved relations with Peking.[67]

The 1974 subcontinental settlement of the prisoners-of-war and displaced populations issues among India, Pakistan, and Bangladesh has created the possibility of significantly reduced tension in that region for the first time since partition. New trade agreements were signed in early 1975, reestablishing economic ties that had been broken a decade earlier. However, in hopes of consolidating India's control in its zone of Kashmir, Mrs. Gandhi reached an agreement in February with the Kashmiri nationalist leader, Sheikh Abdullah,

---

[66] Ibid., p. 156.

[67] Author's interview with U.S. embassy officials, New Delhi, June 1973.

to drop his insistence on a plebiscite in exchange for his appointment as chief minister. Pakistan predictably castigated this development, its reaction fortuitously coinciding with an American decision in March to lift its own decade-old arms embargo to the subcontinent. Commenting on Prime Minister Bhutto's strong protest against the Abdullah-Gandhi agreement, Mrs. Gandhi pointedly noted: "Pakistan's new belligerence coincides with the start of a fresh flow of arms. The meaning of this coincidence should not be lost on the world." [68] Thus, it appeared that Indo-Pakistani tensions were on the rise once more in 1975, despite the settlement of issues which had remained in the aftermath of the 1971 Bangladesh War. But all parties have agreed to Dacca's admission to the United Nations, and the prospect for a new Chinese initiative toward India is perhaps the best it has been in years, particularly if New Delhi provides some evidence— perhaps paradoxically, its nuclear test could be considered as such—of its desire to remain independent of the Soviet Union. Unfortunately, New Delhi's spring 1975 incorporation of Sikkim into the Indian Union once again exacerbated relations with both Peking and Rawalpindi.

The Soviet Asian-collective-security concept remains amorphous more than five years after it was first broached. In that period, Moscow has modified its explanation of the idea from manifest containment of China and replacement of American security guarantees in the region to an appeal for the membership of all Asian states, including China and possibly even the U.S. The Russians have denied that their proposal constitutes a military pact and speak of it rather in terms of a series of nonaggression arrangements encompassing "the renunciation of the use of force in relations between states, respect for sovereignty, and inviolability of frontiers." [69] The one element providing continuity from 1969 through 1974 is Moscow's insistence that its military, economic, and diplomatic presence combined with its geography make it an Asian power. Therefore, the significance of the U.S.S.R.'s Asian collective security idea is to put both the region and the United States on notice that no future political and security arrangements should be made for Asia without Soviet participation and concurrence.

---

[68] *New York Times*, 27 February 1975.
[69] "Live According to the Laws of Peace," *Pravda*, 15 January 1974.

4

THE SPECIAL CASE OF THE TWO KOREAS: OPPORTUNITY LOST?

Background

This study has focused primarily on the security problems of South and Southeast Asia because these include the region in which the United States has been militarily involved over the last decade, the region identified by the ASEAN neutralization proposal, and the areas of major interest to the U.S.S.R. in its notion of Asian collective security. While South and Southeast Asia are prime candidates for significant diplomatic activity during the remainder of this decade, it should be remembered that Northeast Asia has also been affected by the great-power changes described earlier.

This chapter will examine the efforts of the two Koreas to adjust to what has appeared as their allies' possible disengagement from their respective roles as security guarantors. Both Seoul and Pyongyang fear that détente between the United States and China and between the United States and the U.S.S.R. could be effected at the expense of the national goals of each Korea, and both capitals have moved over the last few years to reassert the importance of their alliance relations as well as to open new bilateral dealings with each other.

The intensity of mutual hostility and suspicion that flows between Seoul and Pyongyang can be seen in the combined defense budgets of the two countries, which have been running well over $1 billion annually in the 1970s. This can be compared with the comparable figure for the two Vietnams of approximately $1.6 billion in the midst of a major war.[1] Neither side could sustain either this

---

[1] Charles B. McLane, "Korea in Russia's East Asia Policy," in Young C. Kim, ed., *Major Power and Korea* (Silver Spring, Maryland: Research Institute on Korean Affairs, 1973), p. 4.

heavy a military budget or a major military engagement without the support of its major allies—hence, the concern of each over possible desertion by the superpowers.

While both states are dependent on the United States and the Soviet Union respectively, the Democratic People's Republic of Korea (D.P.R.K.) has been the less successful in diversifying both its political and economic support until recently. Thus, nearly all of North Korea's modern weapons are of Soviet design. And the U.S.S.R. annually accounts for about 70 percent of the D.P.R.K.'s total trade. Moreover, it was Russian economic aid that served to bail out Pyongyang's postponed Seven Year Plan.[2] While heavy material dependence on Moscow has characterized North Korea's external relations, Pyongyang's primary alternative partner has been Peking, which, in 1971, signed its first military assistance agreement with the D.P.R.K. since 1956.

For China, North Korea's importance is enmeshed in the Sino-Soviet confrontation. Geographically, of course, the D.P.R.K. abuts the Manchurian border which now—just as in 1950—comprises one of the most important industrial centers of the country. Moreover, literally hundreds of thousands of Koreans reside in northeast China. A North Korea aligned exclusively with Moscow could pose a serious security threat. Hence, Chou En-lai has carefully cultivated North Korea's Premier Kim Il-sung since the winding down of China's Cultural Revolution in 1969.

North Korea itself has encouraged a Sino-Soviet competition for its "affections." As early as 1955, Premier Kim had decided that it was unwise to become totally dependent on either giant Communist neighbor. And he gradually eliminated those factions in the Korean Workers' party (KWP) identified with either Moscow or Peking. Moreover, Kim's view of the U.S.S.R.'s reliability became somewhat jaundiced after the Russian backdown in the 1962 Cuban missile crisis, when he began to take the Chinese side of the rapidly accelerating polemic between China and Russia, insisting on the priority of support for revolution over nuclear détente.

North Korea's pro-China "tilt" was corrected, however, when the Cultural Revolution led to some Red Guard jibes at Kim Il-sung as a corpulent revisionist. More important than the personal insult against "the beloved leader of the Korean people" was a growing fear of China's unreliability in the throes of its domestic upheavals. Just as the Cultural Revolution waned and it appeared that China was

---

[2] Ibid., p. 10.

approaching the D.P.R.K. once again with security assistance against a possible remilitarized Japan, the political ground again moved under Kim Il-sung's feet. First the United States and then Japan effected rapid détentes with Peking between the Kissinger visit of July 1971 and the Chou-Tanaka communiqué of September 1972. While there might be a silver lining in the Sino-U.S. détente if it could lead to increased pressure on the Americans to remove their troops from the Korean peninsula, Pyongyang viewed the development as generally inimical to its intentions toward Seoul insofar as détente appeared to weaken China's support for these intentions (to be discussed below).

Although over the past several years the R.O.K. has managed to diversify its economic relations and, to an extent, its political ties, it has, nonetheless, been dependent on the security guarantees of a major power, as has its northern antagonist. As Bernard Gordon has pointed out, America's initial decision to defend South Korea in 1950 was not so much a product of the country's intrinsic value to the United States as it was a conclusion that the Korean peninsula must not be occupied by a power hostile to Japan.[3] Thus, the commitment to Japan's defense led to a corollary commitment to the R.O.K. Although the original strategic importance of the Korean peninsula to the defense of Japan has diminished with the growth of nuclear weaponry, the American commitment to South Korea's survival remains. Through the 1950s and 1960s, this commitment was part of a global containment posture. But in the mid-1970s a new rationale and substance for the R.O.K.-U.S. relationship is being sought. In this quest, Japan's role once more looms large. Its trade, investment, and tourism ties to South Korea have been widely noted. And the argument could be made that if the R.O.K. were lost to a hostile North Korea, although Japan's strategic situation may not change, Tokyo, nevertheless, could become economically, politically, and psychologically isolated in Northeast Asia—its historical sphere of influence and operations.

R.O.K. leaders began to search for political diversification as early as the Johnson presidency. The formation of ASPAC in 1966 served to broaden Seoul's non-Communist political ties. And the Sato-Nixon communiqué in 1969 was an abortive American attempt to involve an East Asian power in Korea's defense. Soon after Nixon's Guam speech, Vice-President Agnew visited the R.O.K. and

---

[3] Bernard Gordon, "Korea in the Changing East Asia Policy of the United States," in Kim, ed., *Major Powers and Korea*, pp. 48–49.

raised the prospect with President Park of removing 20,000 U.S. troops by 1971 and the remainder by 1975, subsequent to the modernization of the R.O.K. armed forces. The five-year modernization plan has not been realized, however, due to congressional budget cuts. In 1973, for example, the Congress appropriated only 60 percent of the requested amount for that year.[4] Therefore, some 38,000 U.S. forces remain in South Korea with no announced plans for their imminent withdrawal.

Until the petroleum crisis of late 1973, the Park regime's political fortunes were augmented by one of the fastest economic growth rates in Asia—per capita income rising by a multiple of 3.5 between 1960 and 1973 or from $90 to $320.[5] The rate of inflation was low, moreover, as government restrictions on wage rates and trade union activity kept a brake on labor costs. Combined with a strong entrepreneurial spirit and government direction of investment (substantially from overseas), the low-cost, plentiful, and disciplined labor force spurred what has perhaps been the most spectacular example of export-led economic growth yet seen. Exports during the 1962–72 period rose at an annual rate of 40 percent. By 1973, they were valued at $3.1 billion as compared with a 1961 base of $41 million.

Foreign capital accounted for about 40 percent of total annual investment through 1973, of which Japan holds the lion's share of $512 million. But dependence on exports for growth can be a tricky business since mounting export demands have required even larger increases in imports to supply industry with materials and equipment. In addition, heavy reliance on exports means the country is running the risk of being severely hit by currency changes as world money rates sway erratically. Moreover, high defense spending (20–30 percent of the national budget) limits the government's ability to replace foreign investment, which began to diminish after the October 1973 Middle East War. Thus, by the end of that year, Seoul faced a potential economic downturn for the first time in well over a decade, as exports began to dwindle and Japanese investment and tourism slowed.[6]

---

[4] Figures cited in Young-whan Kihl, "The Nixon Doctrine and South-North Korean Relations," *Korean Journal of International Studies*, vol. 4, nos. 3-4 (October 1973), pp. 107–108.

[5] This discussion is drawn from the excellent article by Tony Patrick, "Park Tenses for the Challenge," *Far Eastern Economic Review*, 7 January 1974, pp. 36–39.

[6] Sungjoo Han, "South Korea: The Political Economy of Dependency," *Asian Survey*, vol. 14, no. 1 (January 1974), p. 51.

The Koreas' Views of Each Other

South Korean officials explain that although President Park had originally believed unification could not be discussed with North Korea until the late 1970s, the timetable was accelerated because of the unexpected rapidity of R.O.K. economic growth and because of the changes in the international environment resulting from the Nixon Doctrine, Sino-U.S. and Soviet-U.S. détente, and Japan's normalization of relations with China. The North Koreans' willingness to respond to what R.O.K. authorities claim was their initiative for bilateral talks (the D.P.R.K. claims the reverse) occurred because Pyongyang similarly feared a negative change in the environment as its major backers worked out a modus vivendi with the American enemy. Additionally, the South Koreans continue, North Korea had seen that its use of violence to precipitate southern unrest in the late 1960s had proved counter-productive, actually serving to build up and modernize the R.O.K. armed forces with U.S. assistance. Perhaps a change in tactics to peaceful negotiations could cause both the R.O.K. and the United States to lower their military guard and accelerate American withdrawal.[7] Particularly noteworthy in these views is the belief that Pyongyang was essentially uninterested in a reduction of tensions between the two Koreas and perceived bilateral discussions between itself and Seoul as simply another means of weakening South Korea in order to obtain unification on its terms. Derivatively, North Korea's international image would benefit from an apparent willingness to negotiate directly with South Korea, permitting it to emerge from a largely self-imposed isolation which had confined it to the Communist community. This benefit did indeed accrue to Pyongyang as it broadened its international memberships in 1973 to include WHO, UNCTAD, the IPU, and permanent observer status in the United Nations.

North Korea's first proposal for a peaceful confederation was broached in August 1960. At that time Kim Il-sung suggested that each side retain its political system and cooperate in the economic and cultural spheres. Kim's proposal coincided with the brief Chang government which, of all R.O.K. governments before and since, was the most interested in exploring unification possibilities. Chang's replacement by General Park in 1961, however, was followed by a comparable hardening of northern tactics and an appeal by Kim Il-sung in September of that year for the formation of a southern

---

[7] Author's discussion with members of the National Unification Board, Seoul, 10 May 1973.

revolutionary party, whose task would be to pave the way for unification by seizing power, forcing the withdrawal of American forces, and then moving toward "peaceful unification." [8]

The 4 July 1972 joint communiqué of North and South Korea, which set up provisions for political negotiations between the two sides for the first time, was greeted euphorically by a number of observers. One referred to it as amounting to a "virtual nonaggression pact" and "*de facto* recognition" of the legitimacy of each other's regimes with the promise of an end to mutual vituperation and a cessation of military incidents.[9] But even these initial high hopes were tempered by the fact that each side's interpretation of the communiqué's meaning was diametrically opposed—North Korea claiming that unification must be achieved completely without outside assistance and South Korea insisting that the United Nations could not be regarded as an "outside force." [10] Nor was there any indication that Kim Il-sung would repudiate his support for the revolutionary party in the South. R.O.K. officials pointed out that concurrent with the 4 July communiqué, Radio Pyongyang broadcast a program stressing that peaceful unification could only follow a successful South Korean revolution—hardly a viewpoint designed to instill confidence in the Park government. And, only a little more than a year later, Kim Il-sung stated to Australian leftist journalist Wilfred Burchett that the joint talks were meaningless as long as Park remained president of the R.O.K.[11]

In hopes of undermining or at least embarrassing the Park government, the KWP issued an appeal on 16 November 1973 for the convocation of "a great national congress consisting of representatives of the people of all walks of life, political parties, and public organizations in the North and South." In order for such a conclave to occur, the KWP averred, "the South Korean authorities must stop all manner of suppression of the popular masses in South Korea, release the arrested and detained democratic figures and patriotic students and guarantee the freedom of activities for national reunification to the people of all walks of life." [12] In effect, Kim was

---

[8] A useful resume of the 1960s may be found in Rinn-Sup Shinn, "North Korean Policy toward South Korea," in Kim, ed., *Major Powers and Korea*, pp. 89–90.

[9] Young-whan Kihl, "Korean Response to Major Power Rapprochement," in Kim, ed., *Major Powers and Korea*, p. 152.

[10] B. C. Koh, "North Korea: A Breakthrough in the Quest for Unity," *Asian Survey*, vol. 13, no. 1 (January 1973), p. 85.

[11] Letter from R.O.K. Consul Won Chang in Hong Kong, published in the *Far Eastern Economic Review*, 1 October 1973, p. 6; and Wilfred Burchett, "A Talk with Kim Il-sung," *Far Eastern Economic Review*, 10 September 1973, p. 27.

[12] KWP statement, carried by the Korean Central News Agency, 16 November 1973.

trying to use the reunification talks to buttress the position of Park's opponents and hopefully bring pressure to bear for the abolition of anti-Communist and national security laws, which, in turn, would facilitate Communist infiltration.

Radio Seoul charged that the Pyongyang had broken the 4 July communiqué promise against slanderous broadcasts as early as February 1973, and that by June its Voice of the Revolutionary Party for Reunification was beaming seditious material to South Korea six hours per day. At the same time, according to Radio Seoul, North Korea reinstituted military probings along the armistice line.[13]

In December 1973, North Korea suddenly claimed jurisdiction of the waters surrounding a number of small islands off Korea's west coast above the thirty-eighth parallel that were awarded to the R.O.K. in the 1953 armistice agreement. In February 1974, the D.P.R.K. Navy seized South Korean fishing vessels that were allegedly engaged in espionage operations in this area. The R.O.K. threatened retaliation, but the situation ultimately cooled.[14] Pyongyang, however, had clearly warned Seoul that the military situation had deteriorated to the pre–4 July communiqué level.

At the United Nations, in his first address to the General Assembly in his new role of permanent observer, the D.P.R.K. representative revealed his country's primary purpose in broaching the communiqué on unification: to create a situation in which "it is necessary, first of all, to put an end to the interference of outside forces."[15] With disarming simplicity, the delegate opined:

> When the foreign troops pull out of South Korea, there will remain only the armed forces of the North and the South. In this case, since there exists the North-South joint statement in which the North and South have pledged not to fight with each other, . . . the North-South joint statement will reliably guarantee peace in Korea so long as the South Korean authorities do not violate it.[16]

Negotiations at the United Nations led to the consensual abolition of the twenty-year-old United Nations Commission for the

---

[13] Statement by R.O.K. Culture and Public Information Minister Yun Chu-yong, broadcast by the Seoul Domestic Service, 5 January 1974.

[14] Park Chong-hui press conference carried by the Seoul Domestic Service, 18 January 1974; and Defense Minister Su Chong-Chol's warning to the D.P.R.K. carried in *Haptong*, 16 February 1974.

[15] D.P.R.K. representative Yi Chong-mok's address to the U.N. General Assembly, KCNA, 16 November 1973.

[16] Ibid.

Unification and Rehabilitation of Korea as no longer necessary because of the direct talks. But Pyongyang was unable to achieve a similar dissolution of the UN Command, as both the R.O.K. and United States effectively argued that without satisfactory alternative security arrangements, the command's withdrawal would be militarily destabilizing. Also against the United States and the R.O.K., the D.P.R.K. refused to consider the simultaneous entry of the two Koreas into full United Nations membership, insisting instead (quite unrealistically but consistent with its emphasis on the priority of unification) that Korea should join the UN only as a single unit.[17]

Until January 1974, diplomatic initiatives in Korean relations appeared to be entirely at North Korea's behest. Then, in a new year's news conference, Park took a leaf out of North Korean diplomacy of the 1950s and called for a nonaggression pact between the two sides. This appeal was clearly consistent with the 4 July joint statement. But once again the high degree of mutual hostility was underlined by North Korea's rejection of Park's proposal. Charging that "the so-called 'nonaggression pact' " was "devoid of any substantial points guaranteeing the country's peace," North Korean media insisted that the pact was a fraud, designed to rationalize the retention of U.S. forces in South Korea and artificially separating "peace from the question of national reunification."[18] The argument was very revealing for it demonstrated that peace was not the priority objective for North Korea; rather it was reunification on Pyongyang's terms.

Dramatizing its contention that the primary obstacle to reunification lay in the American military presence, North Korea's parliament (the SPA) proposed that Pyongyang sign a peace agreement directly with the United States, since it was "well known" that the Americans controlled all military decisions south of the thirty-eighth parallel. Such a peace agreement would "put an early end to foreign interference in our internal affairs."[19] The United States, of course, refused to respond to the North Korean gambit, but the proposal had served its purpose of publicizing the fact that only South Korea had retained foreign troops on its soil since 1958. And if these developments were not clear enough, *Nodong Sinmun* stated baldly on 16 June 1974 that "the purpose of the [North-South] dialogue is to

---

17 There is a good discussion of these UN developments in the *Far Eastern Economic Review*, 10 December 1973, p. 32.

18 *Nodong Sinmun* editorial, 26 January 1974.

19 Deputy Premier Ho Tam's Report to the SPA, carried by KCNA, 25 March 1974.

reunify the divided country, not to pursue 'peaceful coexistence' while leaving the country divided as it is into the north and the south."

There is some evidence suggesting Peking's possible lack of enthusiasm over this militant North Korean stance. In a commentary ostensibly criticizing U.S. military aid to Taiwan, *Nodong Sinmun* draws an implicit parallel between the U.S. "occupation" of Taiwan and its role in South Korea. By implication chiding Peking, the North Korean paper states that continued American military aid to Taiwan "discloses the black-hearted design of the U.S. imperialists not to withdraw from Taiwan but keep their hold on this island as their colony and military base and step up their policies of aggression and war against the Chinese people and the Asian people. *This is a challenge to the Chinese people and the Asian people.*" (Emphasis added.) [20]

The thrust of the foregoing discussion is that North Korea's willingness to enter into direct negotiations with South Korea has not been the result of a change in Pyongyang's objectives: (1) to force the exit of the U.S. military and (2) to effect reunification under Communist aegis. Rather, détente was a calculated change in tactics to increase world (and American) public opinion pressure to effect some change in the stalemated peninsular situation. Moreover, this tactical change can be traced back as far as Kim Il-sung's 6 August 1971 speech—less than one month after the announcement of Nixon's impending visit to China—in which the North Korean leader stated Pyongyang's willingness to negotiate directly with the Park government. This initial gambit was followed in January 1972 when, in an interview for Tokyo's *Yomiuri*, Kim appeared to offer an important concession to move the Korean situation off dead center: U.S. troops might be withdrawn *after* the two Koreas had signed a peace pact and agreed to nonaggression.[21] The 4 July joint statement, six months later, was apparently viewed by Kim as fulfilling that concession, however, for North Korea has been pressuring for an American withdrawal once again as its highest priority objective.

When it appeared that South Korea was not about to accede to Pyongyang's scenario and as the Park regime cracked down on domestic dissenters, North Korea abruptly changed its posture. By July 1973, the joint meetings were suspended by Pyongyang amidst charges against Seoul that the South Korean Central Intelligence Agency was participating in and obstructing the talks and that the

---

[20] *Nodong Sinmun*, 13 May 1974.

[21] Shinn, "North Korean Policy toward South Korea," p. 102.

Park regime's repression of student dissent rendered Seoul an inappropriate location for the conduct of negotiations.[22]

When the North-South Committee finally reconvened in late January 1974 at Panmunjom, Kim Il-sung's delegates insisted that South Korea broaden its membership to include some "60 to 70" political organizations as well as overseas Koreans. Pyongyang went on to reject Park's call for a north-south nonaggression pact which, according to the D.P.R.K., would simply legitimize the division of the country and the continued presence of U.S. forces.[23] And at a Pyongyang rally on 4 March for visiting Algerian President Boumedienne, Kim took the occasion to express "positive support" for "the revolutionary struggle of the South Korean people" which, according to Seoul's minister of culture and information, revealed that North Korea had completely scrapped the 4 July statement. Soon thereafter, North Korean media acknowledged that the South Koreans arrested as members of a Communist subversive organization in Seoul did, indeed, belong to a local revolutionary party. Whether true or not, such a cynical admission obviously sealed their fate and served to keep the pot of civil unrest boiling below the 38th parallel.[24] Since the Park government would not agree to Pyongyang's terms of negotiation, the latter would continue to support South Korea's "patriotic revolutionary struggle . . . to achieve national reunification." [25]

By the spring of 1974 it appeared that Pyongyang had lost interest in the reunification talks. In a program for domestic audiences, Radio Pyongyang stated:

> It is obvious that the dialogue for national reunification cannot progress smoothly as long as we deal with the Pak Chong-hui clique, a despicable traitorous clique. That is why we have proposed that members of the South Korean delegation to the NSCC be replaced by patriots desiring unification; that the machinery of the NSCC be enlarged and that, separate from the present NSCC, a great national assembly, or a north-south political consultative conference consisting of representatives of political parties, public organizations, and people of all walks of life north and south be convened as soon as possible.[26]

22 Typical is the KCNA dispatch of 28 November 1973.

23 KCNA, 31 January 1974.

24 KCNA, 16 March 1974.

25 *Minju Chosen* Commentator, 29 March 1974.

26 Pyongyang Domestic Service in Korean, 3 May 1974.

For North Korea, then, the primary benefit from the relatively shortlived thaw in relations with South Korea is found in the international sphere. The demise of the Hallstein doctrine for Korea has created new opportunities for Pyongyang in countries where heretofore only Seoul had been represented. Perhaps the best illustration of this is Pyongyang's new contact with Tokyo. The purpose behind the creation of a new Japan-D.P.R.K. relationship, initiated in 1971 with invitations to Japanese political, press, and business delegations, was to diversify trade away from such heavy dependence on the U.S.S.R. and China and to weaken any Japanese thought of taking the place of the United States in the military defense of South Korea. An initial trade agreement was signed in January 1972, and by the end of 1973, two-way trade had grown by 23 percent. Expectations for 1974 were even higher, because the Japanese government agreed to permit the use of Export-Import Bank loans to finance exports to North Korea. This decision cleared the way for the sale of a $150 million cement plant in 1973 and led to a North Korean offer to purchase some 500,000 tons of steel products in 1974.[27]

While détente appeared to put Pyongyang on the offensive in peninsular politics, for the Park regime it has proved a mixed and worrisome blessing. It has placed Seoul on the defensive in external affairs, for the R.O.K. prefers to maintain the division of the country. For Park personally, however, the necessity of dealing with North Korea in sensitive political negotiations provided an excuse to strengthen his powers through the declaration of a state of emergency and to suppress student and intellectual opinion which had been pressing for greater civil liberties and political participation.

Just as Pyongyang has sought to break out of its Communist diplomatic enclave to improve its international respectability, so has Seoul essayed new contacts with such hitherto anathema capitals as Moscow and Peking. In September 1971, Park announced a willingness to have the R.O.K. establish diplomatic relations with the two Communist giants, even before President Nixon's journey to Peking.[28] Although Peking has ignored South Korean overtures, it is noteworthy that Moscow, beginning in the spring of 1973, permitted a South Korean artist and two businessmen to visit the Soviet Union, followed by an invitation for South Korean participation in the fall 1973 Moscow Universiad sports competition.[29]

[27] *Kyodo* (Tokyo), 26 January 1974.
[28] Kihl, "Korean Response," p. 142.
[29] Kihl, "The Nixon Doctrine and Korean Relations," pp. 116–117.

Although it appeared for a time in late 1973 that President Park might be willing to compromise with student civil-liberties demands when, in response to their protests, he dismissed Lee Hu-rak, the head of the South Korean CIA, the hope proved shortlived when, in January 1974, he instituted a new series of "emergency measures," virtually abolishing freedom of the press (or anyone else for that matter) to criticize the government.[30] International revulsion against Park's crackdown has not only weakened the distinction and appeal of South Korea's alternative to North Korean communism, but it has created a general lack of trust by South Koreans in their own government and provided a propaganda windfall for the publicists in Pyongyang.[31] Western reports placed the number of those arrested for opposition to the government in the first six months of 1974 as high as 4,000.[32] And in June a trial, clearly designed to associate any opposition to the government with North Korean machinations, was begun in Seoul.[33]

Ways of Limiting Conflict

U.S. forces have been stationed in Korea since 1945. America fought its second most unpopular war there between 1950–1953. And the prospect for an American withdrawal remains dim so long as the North Koreans maintain their belligerent posture and the R.O.K. government continues to call for U.S. steadfastness. Indeed, by mid-1974, Washington had actually slightly increased the number of airmen in South Korea, to bring the total number of U.S. forces there close to 40,000.[34]

If the U.S. government would fulfill its 1969 pledge to fully modernize the R.O.K. forces, then, a number of analysts argue, Washington should be able to withdraw all ground forces from Korea, since it was demonstrated in Vietnam that Korean divisions fight as effectively as their American counterparts—at one-tenth the cost. A modernized R.O.K. Army with U.S. air support should be a sufficient deterrent against attack from the D.P.R.K.[35] Such a develop-

---

[30] The emergency decrees were carried by *Haptong* on 8 January 1974.

[31] See the interview with opposition leader Kim Tae-chung in the *Far Eastern Economic Review*, 29 April 1974.

[32] *New York Times*, 16 June 1974.

[33] *Haptong*, 17 June 1974.

[34] Christian Muller, "Korean Confrontation," *Swiss Review of World Affairs*, June 1974, p. 21.

[35] Gurtov, "Security by Proxy."

ment should be distinguished from a complete withdrawal from Korea and the termination of any American commitment there, however. Although a number of observers have recommended precisely that approach for Indochina, few have done so for Korea. Rather, there is a belief among Asian security analysts that the U.S. commitment to the R.O.K. is an important psychological buttress to Japan's confidence in its U.S. Mutual Security Treaty *despite* the fact that Korea no longer represents a real strategic threat to Japan.[36] A U.S. withdrawal, it is held, would create a dangerous "vacuum," which China, Japan, and the Soviet Union would all compete to fill.[37] Moreover, China, at least, may well tacitly prefer the maintenance of a U.S. presence in South Korea after the Shanghai communiqué formalized America's nonaggressive intentions. A continued U.S. presence would maintain the peacefulness of China's Korean border, whereas a new Korean war—following a U.S. withdrawal—would direct Chinese attention away from its northern border with the U.S.S.R.[38]

South Korean analysts are quick to point out that the D.P.R.K. holds a five-to-one advantage in both sea and air power and is capable of producing most of its own armaments. By contrast, the R.O.K. began to manufacture the basic infantry M-16 rifle only in 1973, the same year its first steel mill went into production. R.O.K. analysts have suggested that if North Korea would be willing to accept the legitimacy of an American troop presence in South Korea, then Seoul would be willing to discuss the mutual reduction of defense expenditures and military establishments. But, according to these same observers, none of these issues has even been raised at the reunification talks.[39]

At present, North Korea appears adamantly opposed to a "German solution" of the Korean problem, that is, international formalization of the peninsula's division, while the Park government is equally intransigent against any meaningful political relations between the two. Yet each remains concerned about the reliability of its backers whom, since 1971, they have witnessed arriving at a number of bilateral understandings.

---

[36] Clough, "East Asia," p. 55.

[37] Robert E. Osgood, "How New Will the New American Foreign Policy Be?" in John H. Gilbert, ed., *The New Era in American Foreign Policy* (New York: St. Martin's, 1973).

[38] Harold Hinton, "Chinese Policy toward Korea," in Kim, ed., *Major Powers and Korea*, pp. 24–25.

[39] Author's discussions at the National Unification Board and the Asiatic Research Center of Korea University, 10 May 1973.

Seoul has expressly objected to American proposals for the redeployment of its Korean forces to the central Pacific, for fear that they would not remain an effective deterrent so far away from Korean soil.[40] (The parallel to U.S. troops in Western Europe is obvious.) Pyongyang, on the other hand, has attempted to encourage such a redeployment of forces by proposing directly to the United States (bypassing the R.O.K.) a military armistice agreement and offering a nonaggression pledge in exchange for the withdrawal of American forces.[41]

Unless Pyongyang recognizes the Park government's authority to negotiate questions of tension reduction, there is no hope for détente on the peninsula. The 4 July 1972 statement was so hopeful precisely because it appeared to grant mutual legitimacy. By 1974, however, relations had deteriorated to the pre-4 July level, in part at least because North Korea had calculated that Park's own heavy-handed political tactics had undercut his support and increased the probability of a popular uprising against his government. The irony of these negative developments is that they are really counter-productive for both sides; for if they could agree to some sort of modus vivendi, they could reduce their dependence upon outsiders. But so long as they fuel mutual hostility, outside allies remain essential because neither could deter or fight without them.

From the perspective of American policy, a key question is whether there is a way in which the United States can simultaneously assure South Korea of its protection against North Korean aggression while communicating to Pyongyang that American military might, so close to its border, would be reduced. One possibility would be a tacit quid pro quo arrangement whereby U.S. forces were reduced as tensions abated. Such a process would, of course, depend on Kim Il-sung's recognition once more of the legitimacy of a South Korean government. Another possibility would be a reduction in U.S. forces in the R.O.K. but an increase in American investment so that the South Koreans would be assured that the United States had not simply written off their country completely.

For the present, however, the prognosis is not favorable. Had the Park government been characterized by less megalomania and Kim not seized the opportunity to promote revolution once more, the 1972 overtures may have been a major breakthrough in a move-ment toward peaceful coexistence. As it is, Korea is once more in a

---

[40] See the editorial in *Tong-A Ilbo*, carried by *Haptong*, 4 March 1974.
[41] The text of the proposal was carried by KCNA on 25 March 1974.

state of neither peace nor war. An American decision to withdraw forces unilaterally in this context could be highly destabilizing. But efforts once again to seek effective bases for détente should not abate, both for the sake of the two Koreas and to reinforce America's broader policy of tension reduction in Northeast Asia.

5
ASIAN SECURITY FOR THE LATE 1970s

The Search for Small Power Self-Reliance

From the perspective of Asian small and middle powers, the quest for international security in the late 1970s will probably involve regional efforts to isolate the great powers from local quarrels. Neutralization, if honored by the major powers, is one way of achieving this end. Another way might be regional small-state alliances designed to cope with local conflicts in such a way that external intervention would be minimized. Examples of local cooperation on security matters abound in Southeast Asia, as, for example, on the Malaysian-Indonesian and Malaysian-Thai borders, where neighboring states have institutionalized the monitoring and control of insurgent activity.[1] There are, on the other hand, several counterexamples of Asian border insurgencies where effective cooperation has not been arranged: India-Burma, Indonesia-Philippines, and Philippines-Malaysia—the latter two cases concerning Muslim unrest in the southern Philippines and the former, India's Naga rebels, who pass through Burma between India and China. One could add to these the incipient threat induced by the presence of ethnic Vietnamese on the northern and northeastern Thai borders with Laos, particularly since the Pathet Lao now have direct access to the Thai border through the new Pathet Lao-dominated government.

---

[1] Malaysian-Thai border-security cooperation should be qualified, however, by Thai suspicions of certain Malay fundamentalist political leaders' irredentist motives toward the Muslim community in the southern Thai provinces. In this particular region, the Thais may be more concerned with Muslim separatism than they are about the Communists, whom they regard more as a threat to Malaysia than to themselves.

Implicit in the foregoing discussion is the existence of two separate but potentially interconnected security challenges to Asian governments. One is concerned with great-power competition for regional allegiance and resources. The other is a part of the unsettled political order of the region itself and concerns both ethnic autonomy demands (southern Thailand, southern Philippines) and latent irredentism (the Philippines claim to Sabah, possible Vietnamese designs on northern Thailand, the Pakistani claim to Kashmir), as well as competing ideological claims to political power represented by leftist challenges to the incumbent order. The greatest danger to Asia lies in a linkage of these two types of challenge, as, for example, if Peking were to greatly increase its military assistance to the Kachin and Shan rebellions in Burma and simultaneously attempt to establish a sphere of influence across the Burmese border south of Yunnan province.

The creation of reasonably stable external relations with Asia, then, is rendered doubly difficult by the temptation of outside powers to deal with political challengers rather than incumbents in many countries. Some analysts have gone so far as to argue that no externally imposed regional balances can be effectively struck until the ethnic and elite challenges endemic to Asia are worked out (at times violently) by the Asians themselves.[2] The great powers may be able to reduce the scale of violence involved in regional conflicts by limiting the available weaponry, but it is unlikely that they can eliminate the violence entirely without politically unacceptable intervention. Therefore, the problem boils down to the limitation and isolation of regional violence so that opportunities and incentives for great power intervention are reduced to the lowest possible level.

Because small states are unable to control the behavior of their larger brethren, their best opportunity for independence lies in their ability to create regional situations which are viewed by major powers as either so stable or so relatively unimportant that they do not justify the risks of competitive intervention. In effect, small states desire to create a situation in which the major powers do not perceive them as a cockpit of large-state competition.[3] There are two ways of effecting this goal, and each of them presupposes an end to the current alliance arrangements of the third-world Asian states. One approach,

---

[2] George Liska, *States in Evolution: Changing Societies and Traditional Systems in World Politics*, International Affairs Study 19 (Washington, D. C.: Washington Center for Foreign Policy Research, Johns Hopkins University, 1973), p. 62.

[3] David Vital, *The Survival of Small States: Studies in Small Power-Great Power Conflict* (London: Oxford University Press, 1971), pp. 6–7, 9.

presently advocated by Singapore, is a multiple access strategy in which all states are given equal opportunity to engage in a variety of relations with the region's members from international trade and investment to military aid and training. This approach presumes that each of the region's members is stable enough to control externally generated activities within its borders so that they benefit rather than undermine the host country. A problem with the multiple access approach, however, is that it may be mistaken for a kind of quadrilateral balance, equating what are, in reality, highly disparate relationships established by each major power with the region's members.[4] Multiple access would also appear to encourage outside intervention in the region's ethnic and elite conflicts mentioned above.

The opposite of a multiple access approach to regional independence is some version of nonalignment, possibly *unguaranteed* by outsiders, since guarantees carry within themselves the seeds of renewed intervention. Such a nonalignment agreement could be a variant of the ASEAN neutralization proposal. It would exclude its members from security ties with outsiders, subject to *regional* verification machinery.[5] Although this approach would permit the purchase of military technology from abroad, it would nevertheless prohibit external intervention in cases of regional violence. The success of *unguaranteed* neutralization depends, in turn, on a congruence between the goals of regional states and those external actors with interests in the region. The latter must feel confident that their interests are not threatened by the policies of independent regional actors. Thus, a conflict may well be brewing between the major maritime states and some ASEAN members (Indonesia, Malaysia, and perhaps the Philippines) over whether the Straits of Malacca will remain an international waterway. Should the littoral states attempt to enforce a national-waters policy, the possibility of great-power intervention grows, regardless of regional neutrality claims.

It should be noted at this point how the concept of nonalignment itself has changed over the past twenty years. No longer does it refer primarily to remaining aloof from the American and Soviet alliance systems. Rather, it has expanded to include the preservation of national independence or regional integrity against inordinate reliance on any outside major power. Thus regional organizations no longer require a specific enemy or threat against which to organize. Instead,

---

[4] Phillip Darby, "Stability Mechanisms in Southeast Asia, II," *International Affairs* (London), vol. 49, no. 2 (April 1973), p. 209.

[5] Ibid., pp. 217–218.

they have come into existence to enhance mutual trust and cooperation and reduce dependence on *all* outsiders.[6]

The diminution of threat-based incentives for regional organization suggests the deradicalization of such hitherto revisionist states as the Soviet Union and China. At least one of the important differences between the operation of SEATO from the mid-1950s to 1970 and that of ASEAN in this decade is the generally altered view of both China and the Soviet Union's regional intentions. Whereas SEATO existed to obstruct presumably predatory behavior, ASEAN seems prepared to offer both Peking and Moscow a stake in the current system insofar as it is the first non-Communist Asian political organization not directed *against* Communist states. Both SEATO and ASPAC (the Asia-Pacific Council, organized in 1966 as another specifically anti-Communist grouping) are atrophying. An anti-Communist basis for regional political consultation is clearly no longer sufficient.

Instead, ASEAN's viability is at least partly attributable to its functional approach to regional needs, arranging its activities through eleven permanent committees which deal regionally with a wide range of issues, running the gamut from tourism through planned regional industrial investment to avoid costly product redundance for small markets. ASEAN political consultations occur regularly at the foreign ministers' meetings. And the five members form a caucusing group in the United Nations system of international organizations. ASEAN deals as a unit with the EEC and maintains a permanent representative in Brussels; it also coordinates member positions on GATT negotiations. The success of these activities could be crucial to the organization's further functional expansion, for its attempt to deal with other international bodies will demonstrate whether the five members can obtain a better outcome by bargaining as a unit than they can individually.

ASEAN's modest but consistent success since its 1967 formation has led to a new controversy among its five members: whether to expand membership to include other Southeast Asian states. Thailand and Malaysia raised the possibility in 1973 as a means of establishing a broader Southeast Asian spectrum. In part the proposal for adding states to ASEAN reflected Burma's interest in membership, and in part it reflected a general feeling among ASEAN members that the organization, as presently constituted, was not involved in helping to settle such major regional problems as the aftermath of the Indochina

---

[6] Author's interview with Singapore officials, 6 June 1973.

war. Thailand, particularly, argued that if ASEAN became involved in postwar Indochina reconstruction, the organization's presence could help to change the framework of international involvement from the globe to the region.[7]

Those who are less enthusiastic about either expanded membership or a greater regional political role fear that ASEAN could be irreparably weakened at this stage of its development by prematurely grappling with political issues (Indochina) over which it has no effective leverage or adding new members whose own severe economic difficulties (for example, Burma) would place an inordinate drain on the organization's diplomatic and economic resources.

Burma's interest in ASEAN is viewed within the region as somewhat idiosyncratic and is posited as having grown out of a reaction to the buildup of Soviet influence in the subcontinent. Given its traditional policy of maintaining good relations with China, one way of avoiding too close an association with a Russian-influenced subcontinent would be to demonstrate adherence to a Southeast Asian regional grouping which has already received Peking's tacit approval.[8]

Parallel with such regional efforts as ASEAN to promote self-reliance are several national foreign-policy postures. Perhaps the most significant is Thailand's because of its recent close reliance on U.S. security arrangements. Bangkok initiated conciliatory gestures toward Peking as early as 1971 with the decision to disarm KMT irregulars operating in northern Thailand.[9] Although American bases provide the country with an annual income of $160 million, this does not represent a significant proportion of Thailand's GNP of close to $8 billion.[10]

As the United States reduces its regional commitments, Thailand has begun to diversify its political contacts. The visit of a North Korean trade delegation in April 1974 was designed to demonstrate the "Thai policy of establishing ties with any country that has no bad intentions toward Thailand, regardless of different systems of government or political doctrine."[11] The indirect target of this action was, of course, North Vietnam.

Moreover, Bangkok has taken a public stance calculated to demonstrate its control over American operations originating in

---

[7] See the report of Thailand's proposal to the Kuala Lumpur ASEAN Foreign Ministers' Conference carried by AFP (Manila), 15 February 1973.

[8] Author's interview with Thai Foreign Ministry Officials, 19 June 1973.

[9] Girling, "A Neutral Southeast Asia?" p. 129.

[10] See the discussion in Shaplen, "Letter from Thailand," p. 83.

[11] Bangkok Domestic Service in Thai, 23 April 1974.

Thailand. Thus, the Thai Foreign Ministry has publicly stated that the United States may not send its Thai-based aircraft for missions in other parts of Asia unless prior permission is granted.[12] And Thailand has intimated on several occasions that American bases would be closed once the D.R.V. demonstrated its intentions to terminate its assistance to the Thai rebels in the north and northeast.[13] Since the final Communist victories in Indochina, the Thais have, of course, called for a complete U.S. military withdrawal by 1976.

A final major example of the search for self-reliance is the effort by many of the littoral states to focus international opinion against a competitive Soviet-American naval arms race in the Indian Ocean. Indian Foreign Minister Swaran Singh probably spoke for most of Asia when he stated to the lower house of Parliament: "Any large scale presence of the navy of one big power is bound to attract navies of other big powers. Such rivalry would create problems for littoral countries, the overwhelming majority of whom desire to maintain the Indian Ocean as an area of peace." [14] Yet the Indian Ocean issue illustrates, perhaps better than any other regional problem, the impotence of Asia when the great powers decide to move militarily into a new area. In the case of the Indian Ocean, both the Nixon Doctrine's dependence on naval mobility and the U.S.S.R.'s overall naval buildup reinforce the potential for naval-arms competition in the region despite (and perhaps because of) the reduction of U.S. air and ground forces in other parts of Asia.

The Questionable Utility of Traditional Security Arrangements

In discussing the prospect of containing hostilities in Korea in Chapter 4, we pointed out that most small-state military conflicts cannot be sustained for long without outside support. Thus, one way of enhancing the probabilities for peace would be a policy by the major arms exporters to put limits on their military assistance and sales to third-world states. Although the U.S. Congress regularly hears advocates of such a policy, their pleas have had little effect. In fiscal 1974, U.S. sales almost doubled to an annual rate of $8.5 billion. Soviet sales in 1973 were estimated at $2 billion, and the figure was the same for U.S. allies, while the Eastern European states sold some $500 million worth of arms to developing countries. Opposition in Congress

---

[12] *The Nation,* 29 March 1974.

[13] A typical statement may be found in *The Nation,* 18 March 1974.

[14] Published in *India News* (Embassy of India, Washington, D. C.), 22 March 1974.

appears to be fading as the Pentagon has shifted from credit to cash payments so that the arms sales are viewed in a fiscal rather than a military-policy context.[15]

A particularly noteworthy example of the importance of the provision of military assistance to the sustenance of military conflict is, of course, the Indochina war. Estimates by the U.S. Department of Defense indicate that between 1966 and 1973, the U.S.S.R. and P.R.C. provided North Vietnam $3.65 billion in military aid—$2.57 billion from Russia and $1.08 billion from China. But over the same period, the United States provided some $107.10 billion to its Indochina allies—a figure including its own military operations. In short, the United States spent twenty-nine times as much for military operations in Southeast Asia as Russia and China together. Even in fiscal 1973, as U.S. aid decreased, it still ran at a rate some eighteen times higher than the two major Communist states. U.S. outlays for Indochina in 1974 have dropped to around $3 billion, but this is still considerably more than the 1973 level of aid by Moscow and Peking. By any criterion the latter have obtained much more cost-effectiveness for a much lower outlay than has the United States. But beyond the fiscal considerations, all three major powers have been instrumental in sustaining the Indochinese bloodshed for over a decade by supporting their clients' military policies rather than exerting pressure through mutually negotiated arms limitations for a political settlement. Moreover, figures prepared by the American intelligence community came to light in March 1975, indicating that Soviet and Chinese aid to Hanoi in 1974 totalled $1.7 billion, exceeding the U.S. aid to Saigon ($1.2 billion) for the same period.[16] The implication is that North Vietnam's successful winter 1975 offensive was made possible by more and better supplies than those available to Saigon. The comparable and simultaneous success of the Communist insurgents in Cambodia may also be due in part to stepped up logistics from Hanoi and Peking.

George Liska cites three reasons for past great-power decisions to align with small states: (1) power aggregation, which is no longer meaningful given the technological base of power in today's international system (for example, the diminishing importance of overseas bases as naval and air technology permit longer cruise periods and faster access to trouble spots); (2) to insure that the small state does not align with an enemy (but nonalignment can serve the same pur-

---

[15] New York Times, 14 July 1974.

[16] Leslie Gelb, "Aid to Hanoi Said to Hit Record and Exceed U.S. Help to Saigon," New York Times, 20 March 1975.

Table 2

MILITARY AID TO SOUTHEAST ASIA, 1966–1973

($ in millions)

Aid Source	1966	1967	1968	1969	1970	1971	1972	1973
U.S.S.R.	500	675	415	175	90	165	375	175
P.R.C.	110	155	115	140	100	115	230	115
Total [a]	610	830	530	315	190	280	605	290
U.S. direct military	5,419	17,262	19,065	19,912	15,941	9,925	5,243	2,995
MASF [b]	393	1,155	947	1,632	1,432	1,527	1,985	2,271
Total [c]	5,812	18,417	20,012	21,544	17,373	11,452	7,228	5,266

[a] Figures for the U.S.S.R. and P.R.C., supplied by Department of Defense, represent total military aid to North Vietnam. Virtually all Russian and Chinese military aid to Indochina was channeled through North Vietnam.

[b] Military Assistance Support Force.

[c] U.S. costs for Southeast Asia from Department of Defense. All figures represent outlays.

pose at a lower cost, assuming the major powers would agree to a halt in competitive alignment policies); and (3) the great power may desire to have a hand in managing local conflicts which it fears could escalate. Recent experience in Southeast Asia, however, suggests that the involvement of great powers in local conflicts almost guarantees their escalation.[17]

One could add to this litany of reasons why previous alliance rationales in the third world are no longer operative the apparent decline of direct Soviet and Chinese military threats along with America's reticence to become involved in another Asian land war. This combination diminishes ally incentives to defer to the preferences of outsiders. Thus, in the long run, the United States may encounter increasing difficulties in maintaining overseas intervention capabilities, especially if the Soviet Union and China comply with a détente scenario. That is, Americans no longer subscribe to a domino theory in Asia; economic aid is no longer viewed as either a development panacea or an effective means of winning allies; and Washington is more concerned with avoiding local conflicts than in joining allies

[17] Liska, *Alliance and the Third World*, pp. 32, 34. See also Rothstein, *Alliances and Small Powers*, p. 19.

who might drag the United States into another regional morass.[18] In other words, both Washington and Moscow may be coming to the conclusion, based on their experiences in the 1960s, that client-states, far from being sources of wealth and prestige, have become claimants on resources and threaten to involve the superpowers in conflicts which are not of their own choosing.

It is perhaps almost banal to reiterate that the United States is in the middle of the process of trying to formulate a new security policy. Containment in Asia has been superseded as a doctrine by the Nixon-Kissinger visits to China and the reconceptualization of the Indochina war as essentially a local rather than a global conflict. But neither U.S. commitments nor military deployment have altered enough to conform to doctrinal change. Although the Pentagon is contemplating a reduction of U.S. forces in Asia—with the partial exceptions of the R.O.K. and Thailand—and a withdrawal to the western Pacific Ocean, some 172,000 U.S. troops still remained in Asia as of mid-1974, a figure roughly comparable to the number stationed there prior to the 1964 buildup.

The key question remains, however: what is the purpose of these forces? To date, the answer is far from clear. One of the Nixon administration's harshest critics has argued that American security policy has been turned on its head. Instead of the classic (and correct) progression from the definition of foreign policy interests, to the formulation of objectives, to the prescription of strategies, and, finally, the calculation of forces and their costs, the U.S. government appears to be operating in reverse: from limited budgets, to trimmed forces, to arbitrary strategies (that is, divorced from political context), leading to the meaningless one-and-one-half-war-capability goal—meaningless, because there is no definition of the types of probable war, their location, or expected allied assistance.[19]

Secretary of Defense Schlesinger appears cognizant of the above criticism of American force planning. In his fiscal year 1976 report, he attempted to address the relationship between conventional-force planning and U.S. political interests in Asia. The report is noteworthy for its focus on northeast Asia—"an area where the interests of the United States, the Soviet Union, the People's Republic of China, and

[18] For analyses consonant with this view, see Samuel Huntington's article in Robert E. Hunter and John E. Reilly, eds., *Development Today: A New Look at U.S. Relations with the Poor Countries* (New York: Praeger, 1972); and Robert W. Tucker, *A New Isolationism: Threat or Promise* (New York: Universe Books, 1972).

[19] Earl C. Ravenal, "The Nixon Doctrine, Defense Policy, and China," in Ravenal, ed., *Peace with China?* pp. 21–41.

Japan converge." Schlesinger particularly stresses the importance of Japan and Korea, where American mutual defense relationships could serve to deter adventurous activities by North Korea or presumably, despite détente, even China or the U.S.S.R. While Schlesinger admits that the size of American forces in Asia would be limited, thus keeping deployment costs down, he does not specify the kinds of contingencies foreseen or the appropriateness of the forces on station to deal with them. Nor does he attempt to calculate any kind of political probability of their occurrence. These last calculations are essential for effective defense planning, that is, the link between political decisions by potential adversaries to engage in military confrontations and the kinds of defensive forces necessary to deter or defend against such challenges.[20]

Equally important, the generally conservative U.S. Asian military posture of large general-purpose forces tends to gear American planning to set-piece forward defense, presupposing a repetition of the conventional assaults of the Korean War period. By contrast, virtually every analyst of Asian strategy agrees that the Korean War scenario is one of the least applicable to the region.[21] Nevertheless, both U.S. forces on the scene and U.S. military assistance to non-Communist governments in the region remain premised on the assumption of the need for sophisticated, expensive, conventional firepower when security challenges are, in fact, composed of low-level, manpower-intensive insurgencies. The adoption of U.S. military doctrines, and consequently the related organization, equipment, and training, alienates a third-world nation from the defense realities and capabilities facing it. Moreover, the U.S. provision of large-scale military aid also provides incumbent governments with the capability to suppress any dissent, not just that of insurgents.

U.S. military assistance programs (MAPs) have been based on the belief that recipients' equipment, doctrine, communications, and staff procedures should emulate those of the United States in order to facilitate joint action. But the Nixon Doctrine, inherited by the Ford administration, is no longer proposing joint action but rather self-reliance. Yet the doctrinal basis for the MAP has not changed accordingly. The control of low-level conflict requires not heavily

---

[20] See James R. Schlesinger, *Annual Defense Department Report: FY 1976* (Washington, D. C.: Department of Defense, 5 February 1975), pp. III-9–11.

[21] Most of the material for this section of the chapter is drawn from the excellent RAND monograph by Guy Parker, Steven Canby, A. Ross Johnson, and William B. Quandt, *In Search of Self-Reliance: U.S. Security Assistance to the Third World under the Nixon Doctrine* (Santa Monica: RAND, R-1092-ARPA, June 1973).

Table 3

ALIGNMENT OF U.S. OBJECTIVES, LEVELS OF SECURITY ASSISTANCE, AND LIKELY THIRD WORLD CONFLICTS, UNDER THE NIXON DOCTRINE

Objective	Level of Assistance	Likely Conflict	Degree of U.S. Involvement
Total force planning	Combined force planning	Attack by U.S.S.R. or P.R.C. on U.S. friend or ally	Greatest
Regionalism	Complementary force planning	Attack by a minor Communist power on U.S. friend or ally	
		Attack by Soviet client on U.S. friend or ally	
Self-reliance	Supplementary force planning	Communist-supported insurgency	
		Soviet client-supported insurgency	
		"Home-grown" insurgency	
		Conflict between U.S. friends or allies	Least

Source: Guy Parker et al., *In Search of Self-Reliance: U.S. Security Assistance to the Third World under the Nixon Doctrine* (Santa Monica: RAND, R-1092-ARPA, June 1973), p. 13.

equipped conventional armed forces with long logistical tails but locally billeted light-infantry and paramilitary forces designed to maintain surveillance over and forestall the buildup to a quasi-conventional conflict.[22] The United States can only initiate this change by substituting a broader-based light-infantry force and corresponding doctrines for the heavily mechanized systems designed for U.S. needs on the central front in Europe.

A reduced supply of sophisticated arms to its friends and allies in Asia, without sacrificing more appropriate lower-level assistance, would have the additional benefit of reducing the beliefs of other regional powers that they, too, must acquire heavy weapons.

Perhaps the best way of illustrating the new concept for Asian defense is to quote from the RAND study on its applicability to the

---

[22] Ibid., p. 53.

current defense problems of South Korea against a hypothetical (and unlikely) North Korean–Chinese attack:

> For South Korea, a strategy of forward defense based upon specially designed barrier systems and forces deserves serious consideration as the most advantageous means of slowing or containing the Chinese. South Korea's forward defense is not particularly vulnerable to encirclement and piecemeal destruction (as are those of Soviet neighbors) because of its mountainous terrain, the limited Chinese/ North Korean mechanized/airborne/amphibious capability, and the narrowness of the Korean peninsula. A barrier strategy would (1) hold the Chinese off longer; (2) lose less territory requiring later regaining by an allied counter-offensive; (3) cause greater Chinese casualties because of the repetitive requirement for large infantry assaults against multiple fortified positions; (4) permit the South Koreans to mobilize a much larger wartime force because of lower equipment requirements and simplified military occupational skills; (5) lower U.S. peacetime assistance costs by replacing the need for sophisticated equipment with labor-intensive barriers which can be financed by the South Koreans themselves. . . .
>
> South Korean divisions are currently modeled upon the pre-1957 triangular U.S. infantry division, which of course is not optimized for barrier warfare. It is an all-purpose division that is most appropriate for slow-moving campaigns where set-piece battle techniques of elaborate obstacles and fields of fire can be applied. Such divisions are expensive because of their large supporting artillery, engineer, and logistical requirements. Barrier divisions, on the other hand, can be light infantry equipped with automatic small arms, mortars, and multiple rocket launchers to suppress mass enemy attacks, and specialized antitank units along the few corridors suitable for tank thrusts. These divisions essentially need only to stand and fight and occasionally withdraw or infiltrate behind the next fully manned barrier. . . .
>
> The South Koreans do not need new combat equipment to support a larger number of smaller and lighter defensive divisions. They need a heavier ratio of machine guns and mortars for their units, and they need to replace the obsolete M-1 rifle with the M-16. . . . Those are all relatively inexpensive changes. Moreover, such simple systems require little backup except for wartime resupply.[23]

---

[23] Ibid., pp. 41–42, 47.

The essential point made by this illustration is that the United States can greatly reduce both the cost and profile of its military aid without sacrificing defense capability or deterrence as long as appropriate strategic doctrines are developed for *each* recipient which are context-specific. Such a massive change in U.S. military-assistance practice would, of course, require that the domestic administrative rationale of the present program be scrapped. Currently, most military assistance is viewed by the Pentagon as a convenient way of getting rid of obsolete equipment, with little thought as to whether and how such materiel may fit the defense requirements of the recipients. Increasingly, the equipment is sold to armies abroad—a process which has come to be viewed by the government as more fiscal than military in nature. Moreover, the incentive to clear military inventories in the United States is strong, for the turnover of materiel provides a rationale, in turn, for greater domestic military spending. These are strongly entrenched bureaucratic interests to overcome. The task will not be an easy one. But for policy makers, the basic question should be confronted: is military assistance going to become the lynchpin for a reduced U.S. military profile in Asia, or will it remain an essentially porkbarrel preserve of the Pentagon divorced from strategic thought?

Two defense analysts, Robert Pranger and Dale Tahtinen, have probed even more deeply into the assumptions behind and justifications for U.S. MAPs in a recent study.[24] They argue that the post-World War II, seamless step-by-step escalation model of global U.S. military assistance is both destabilizing and unrealistic in the 1970s, when cold war assumptions of implacable ideological hostility no longer hold. Rather, they propose to substitute a four-phase assistance model for U.S. military aid which would be situation-specific and amenable to American disengagement as the politico-military setting changes.[25] Pranger and Tahtinen believe that military assistance categories should be devised to support "friendly states," that is, those whose interests and policies are minimally congruent with America's. They stress that ideological orientation—the litmus test of previous military assistance recipients—should be only one of several "friendship" criteria; others could be mutual financial, cultural, or trade relationships.[26] As the RAND analysts cited above,

---

[24] Robert J. Pranger and Dale R. Tahtinen, *Toward a Realistic Military Assistance Program* (Washington, D. C.: American Enterprise Institute for Public Policy Research, 1974).

[25] For a diagram of the model which is a variant of some of those seen in comparative foreign policy studies, see ibid., p. 12.

[26] Ibid., p. 31.

Pranger and Tahtinen also reject overweaning MAAG control over military equipment orders for host countries. Instead, they suggest that MAAG operations focus on the kind of defense planning and operations deemed most appropriate for the geographical and cultural setting of the recipient country and the specific threat facing it. By simplifying the quantity and variety of equipment available to a host state, by fitting that equipment much more closely to the indigenous situation and by insuring its *defensive* character, the authors hold that the probability of regional arms races will also be reduced as capabilities diminish.[27] In this author's opinion, however, the success of the kind of program recommended by Pranger and Tahtinen would also depend in large part on reciprocal and complementary behavior on the parts of the Soviet Union and P.R.C. toward their allies.

American disengagement (if not withdrawal) from Southeast Asia along with Sino-U.S. and Soviet-American détente provide the opportunity to probe even more deeply into the rationale for the whole U.S. alliance structure in the region. For the first time since the Korean War, Washington, at least, has the opportunity to question whether it wishes to continue a policy whereby it supports all governments which identify the same enemies as the United States—especially when these "enemies" are establishing new, peaceful relations with America. Or, should the United States now try to associate itself with those Asian governments representing change and a commitment to social justice regardless of their international alignments? These questions go to the heart of the Nixon Doctrine: if a predatory international communism is no longer our dominant view of Asian international politics, then should we not develop a more satisfactory rationale by which to choose which regimes to support under which circumstances?

In a sense, some of these changes are already occurring through a process of international drift. At its September 1973 meeting in New York, SEATO agreed no longer to stress either collective defense against Communist aggression or containment of China, but to shift its focus to the support of "internal security and development programs." An upshot of this decision was the dissolution of SEATO's Military Planning Office. Some analysts have observed that the only real reasons for the organization's continued existence are that it comprises Thailand's only formal external security guarantee and that it remains an institutional justification for a U.S. military presence in the region.[28]

---

[27] Ibid., pp. 42–43.

[28] Frances Starner, "SEATO: Many Happy Returns," *Far Eastern Economic Review*, 22 October 1973, pp. 31–32.

Although the reduction of the number of U.S. bases and personnel in Asia (still not carried very far in 1974) will reduce the credibility of any future intervention, there are a number of political benefits from this policy insofar as a lower American profile contributes to the relaxation of national tensions where U.S. bases had become an opposition focal point, and international tensions where they were viewed as inordinate interference in the processes of regional affairs. A lower U.S. profile may serve to strengthen the nationalist credentials of incumbent leaders who, prior to this change in American policy, were frequently accused of being American puppets.[29]

The attitudes of Southeast Asian leaders toward the retention of American bases vary. Thanat Khoman, currently an advisor to the Thai government, has presented the case against such bases, arguing (1) that they inhibit the development of a rapprochement with North Vietnam, (2) that they adversely reflect on Thai sovereignty, (3) that they encourage foreign subversion on Thai soil, and (4) that since the U.S. Congress has adopted a resolution prohibiting the use of American troops in Southeast Asian fighting, they would be unable to assist Thailand in the event of an attack.[30] While sympathetic to Thanat's position, the Thai government did not go this far until the fall of Indochina, insisting instead that U.S. forces served as a deterrent and as a bargaining lever in future negotiations with Hanoi. They also provided employment opportunities at a time of economic troubles for Thailand.[31] Thanat's position was adopted soon after the Indochinese collapse, however.

Furthermore, in the Philippines, far from a diminution of U.S. base activity, there is talk of doubling the Subic Bay dry-dock capacity, in large part because labor costs are so much lower than in the United States. Navy estimates claim that repairs costing $32 million at Subic Bay would run to more than $220 million in the United States.[32] Moreover, the Marcos government, far from desiring an American withdrawal, wishes to renegotiate the defense treaty whereby U.S. intervention in the event of outside attack would be much more

---

[29] George McT. Kahin, "The Role of the United States in Southeast Asia," in Soon, ed., *New Directions*, pp. 80–81.

[30] *Prachatipati* (Bangkok in Thai), 10 June 1974.

[31] Foreign Minister Charunphan press conference reported in *The Post* (Bangkok), 8 June 1974.

[32] Joseph Lelyveld, "U.S. Military Presence Is in Asia as of Old, but Justification for It Is all New," *New York Times*, 26 June 1974.

automatic, as in Europe.[33] While Indochinese developments have led to Philippine concern over U.S. commitments, base negotiations are continuing. And it appears unlikely to this author that President Marcos will choose to follow the Thai example. At this point, one can only conclude that while traditional military arrangements are being questioned, military complexes in Okinawa, Korea, and the Philippines appear to be healthy, even though facilities in Thailand are being phased out.

The Balance between Outside Access and Domestic Integrity

> It is hard to show that Southeast Asian resources and peoples are of direct importance to the United States today, either in economic terms or in the capacity of Southeast Asia's 200 million people to advance or hinder the purposes of the United States in the world. They may become more important in time, but, given the diversity of peoples and languages, the political fragmentation of the region, and the generally low level of economic and political development, American interests there are likely to expand slowly. For the same reasons, it would be difficult for China or the U.S.S.R. to organize the region so that it would make an important contribution to Chinese or Soviet power.[34]

This assessment, by a former State Department East Asia specialist now with the Brookings Institution, indicates one preference for the downgrading of Asian affairs in American foreign policy priorities. In order to sustain its objective of prohibiting single nation dominance of the region while still maintaining the low military profile of the Nixon Doctrine, the United States should alter its diplomatic posture in the late 1970s from one of encouraging alliances to one of urging the great powers to avoid competitive intervention in a region where political instability is bound to characterize national affairs for some time to come. As the Indonesian economist-statesman, Soedjatmoko, observed: stability at the present level of poverty is unattainable. Therefore, the great powers must be persuaded that instability is local and endemic rather than a product of their rivals' machinations. Only in this manner can a measure of political detachment develop between the major powers

---

[33] Bernardino Ronquillo, "Philippines: Special Ties End," *Far Eastern Economic Review*—America in Asia Focus—1 July 1974, p. 42.

[34] Clough, "East Asia," p. 56.

and Southeast Asia.[35] Although it would be naive to assume that the major powers would suddenly agree to pursue a policy of self-abnegation, it may not be unrealistic to change the terms of competition from arms supplies to the advocacy of differing development and distributive strategies.

This argument does not go so far as to call for an American military withdrawal from Asia. A precipitous military drawdown could be highly destabilizing, encouraging those in the Soviet Union who might be tempted to employ growing Russian military strength at a time the United States appeared to be disengaging. The point is not unilateral disarmament but rather a reciprocated change in emphasis from military to economic types of access which could be beneficial to both the great powers and the region. Insofar as U.S. forces remain in Asia, they would not be part of an obsolete containment doctrine but rather one element in a potentially triangular balance among the United States, the Soviet Union, and China. Chou En-lai understood this shift in military roles when he urged the United States to maintain some military presence in the region.[36]

Given the growing need of developed countries for access to the mineral resources of Asia's developing states, a primary task for the remainder of the 1970s is to create mutual vested interests between countries producing primary products and their consumers. The petroleum experience may provide a guideline for other mineral producers insofar as oil-rich countries are beginning to acquire "downstream investment." That is, oil-producing countries (for example, Iran) have invested in the processing and marketing activities of their buyers (Ashland Oil), thus developing a vested interest in sustaining the flow of petroleum and reaping greater benefits than merely the sale of crude oil.

Over the last ten years American trade with Asia has doubled, while equity investments have grown three-fold to over $3.5 billion, excluding Japan. While much of this is in oil exploration, the bulk is in labor-intensive manufacturing and finance.[37] American oil companies are operating in the Java Sea, the Gulf of Siam, the Sulu Sea off the Philippines, the South China Sea off Vietnam (operations were suspended in April 1975), the Yellow Sea off South Korea, the Gulf of Martaban off Burma, the Taiwan Strait, and the Bay of Bengal.

---

[35] Soedjatmoko, "The Role of the Major Powers in the Asia-Pacific Region," in Soon, ed., *New Directions*.

[36] Tucker, "American Outlook," p. 48.

[37] Joseph Lelyveld, "Military Role of the U.S. in Southern Asia Changes, but the Stakes Remain Large," *New York Times*, 23 June 1974.

The American auto industry is cooperating with the ASEAN to produce and market within the region all-purpose, stripped-down Asian cars. And U.S. commercial banks have gone in to finance much of this activity. According to U.S. Treasury Department figures, 30 percent of American banking activity in Asia is now in the less-developed states.[38] Heavy American investment in such low-skilled assembly-line industries as textiles and electronics have been criticized by social scientists for earning little foreign exchange and for a failure to take local partners or share their technology. But, counters a Philippine official, at least they provide productive employment.[39] In fact, some Asian areas are already going beyond these types of industries by upgrading labor skills to attract more complex manufacturing. This is true of Singapore in its Jurong industrial estate, as well as of Kuala Lumpur and Hong Kong.

The point to be made here is that for the late 1970s investment by such developed countries as the United States, Western Europe, and Japan is seen by many Asian leaders as a kind of functional equivalent to the military ties of an earlier period, insofar as it represents an earnest of the continued importance of Asia to the Western powers and Japan. Moreover, the tentative steps, initiated by ASEAN in 1971, to package and distribute industrial projects among its five members, are dependent for their success on the availability of outside investment and technical assistance, as in the Asian automobile project mentioned above. At the 1974 ASEAN Foreign Ministers Conference it was agreed to investigate the possibilities of implementing the United Nations staff study on ASEAN industrial integration—the first step toward a real common market in that it would create an ASEAN free-trade area for the new enterprises. Moreover, a movement toward ASEAN industrial cooperation will also lead to a more intimate network of working relationships at both the official and business community levels of the five member states.[40]

What about the Soviet Union? How has it altered its access strategy in the light of the new Asian nationalism and the loosening of alliance ties with the West? The less than successful Soviet Asian collective security proposal has already been discussed and dismissed by most Asians as a transparent substitute for the military dependence they are in the process of attempting to reduce. Rather,

---

[38] Ibid.

[39] Ibid.

[40] Some of these new planning contacts among the automotive manufacturers in ASEAN were mentioned to the author in an interview with Mrs. Rosario Manalo, ASEAN minister of the Department of Foreign Affairs, Manila, 25 May 1973.

according to one astute observer of Soviet behavior in Asia, the Russians, too, are emphasizing an economic-access strategy, which differs from the Western trade and investment approach but is designed to promote the development of state sector economies:

> [The Russians'] manifest unwillingness to sponsor military alliances apart from those conceived in the most general terms (such as the Asian regional security pact . . .), and the smallness of their military presence away from their own borders, contrasts with their activity in the trade and aid field to suggest that strategic considerations are not high on their list of priorities. The picture of an "optimal Asia" which they paint in their theoretical journals and attempt to further by their actions since 1953 is one of gradual development under predominantly non-Communist but nationalist and socialist governments of states with mixed economies, but with a large and growing state-owned industrial sector whose existence justifies description of them as "taking the non-capitalist road." [41]

This is not to say that the Soviet Union has jettisoned its Marxist-Leninist conflict-model of world affairs; it is to point out that the particular dynamics of that model—its substantive policies— have changed over time to the point where peaceful coexistence between states is now described as an integral part of the model, but with the proviso that "there can be no peaceful coexistence of ideologies." The latter caveat is designed, of course, to protect the dictatorial position of the party in any Communist state, but should not be interpreted as a desire to replace non-Communist regimes elsewhere.

Adam Ulam argues, for example, that the Soviets are essentially uninterested in establishing Communist regimes in the third world, because demands from such regimes (for example, Cuba, North Vietnam, North Korea) have drained resources away from domestic needs, have not led to overarching Russian influence, and have increased the probability of superpower confrontation. Relations with a friendly non-Communist government are much more satisfactory because the obligations of such friendship are much less.[42]

Indeed, although Soviet policy in South Asia can focus on India, east of the subcontinent it is highly diffuse, having to concern itself primarily with the festering dispute with China, whose own regional

---

[41] Jukes, *The Soviet Union in Asia*, p. 290.
[42] Adam Ulam, *Expansion and Coexistence: Soviet Foreign Policy, 1917–1973* (New York: Praeger, 2d edition, 1974), p. 707.

position has greatly improved since 1971, the continuing Indochinese conflict, and the new, developing economic relationship with Japan in the Soviet Far East.[43] Typical perhaps is Malaysia's policy of welcoming a limited Soviet economic presence to balance those of other outsiders and underline Kuala Lumpur's independence without, at the same time, going out of its way to attract Russian aid. Indeed, complaints from the Malaysian business community about the quality and service problems connected with Russian goods make the sophisticated Western and Japanese products more attractive alternatives in trade competition.[44]

The Asian states themselves are attempting to get more from their economic contacts with outsiders than they have in the past. The shift to a harder bargaining posture was dramatically illustrated by Japanese Prime Minister Tanaka's hostile public reception in much of Southeast Asia during his January 1974 visit because of alleged Japanese exploitative business practices. In some capitals, Tanaka promised to try to rectify these complaints by urging Japanese businessmen to provide more employment opportunities for host country nationals and to open up managerial positions in Japanese companies operating abroad to citizens of those states.[45]

Moreover, with the 1974 ASEAN decision to implement the UN Experts' Report on Industrial Sharing, Southeast Asia is beginning to move beyond nationalism to what may be the first tentative regional economic grouping whereby ASEAN industries will look outward with exports rather than concentrate, as in the past, solely on import substitution. As Singapore Foreign Minister Rajaratnam put it: "ASEAN, with its 208 million population is an attractive base from which to launch export-oriented industries because the ASEAN region is not only rich in raw materials but it is the only organization in Asia seriously promoting regional economic cooperation. . . ."[46]

In summary, it can be argued that the environment for external Asian security has improved by the mid-1970s largely because Western powers have reduced both their plans for military intervention and their regional capabilities for such actions, while the Soviet Union has not significantly increased its military profile in either category. Simultaneously, the ASEAN states and the countries of South Asia are moving to consolidate their political and military self-reliance,

---

[43] See Sheldon W. Simon, "The Japan-China-U.S.S.R. Triangle," *Pacific Affairs* (Summer 1974), for a discussion of the relatively weak Soviet position in East Asia.

[44] Author's interviews in Kuala Lumpur, June 1973.

[45] *Kyodo* report of the Japan-Indonesia joint statement, 17 January 1974.

[46] AFP (Hong Kong), 16 May 1974.

hoping not only to accelerate the departure of Western forces and bases but to demonstrate that the need for such facilities no longer exists as countries of the region, singly and collectively, deal with their own indigenous security problems. The establishment of diplomatic or economic ties with China (and in some cases, North Vietnam) are designed to end the isolation of these governments from their Asian neighbors and to encourage them to reduce their assistance to neighboring insurgencies. Insofar as this assistance was sustained by the presence of U.S. troops, their withdrawal should remove the proximate cause of much regional tension.

Security, then, can be a product of a variety of policies. In times of perceived expansionist action by antagonistic states, military strength and deployment may serve to deter and will certainly serve to defend. But at a time when military action has proved indeterminate, the reduction of forces may serve to lower tensions and hostility, while the maintenance of political and economic access by friendly powers still serves to reassure a regional partner of the continued importance of its national growth and integrity.

Cover and book design: Pat Taylor